# High Performance Responsive Design

*Building Faster Sites Across Devices*

Tom Barker

O'REILLY®    Beijing · Cambridge · Farnham · Köln · Sebastopol · Tokyo

**High Performance Responsive Design**
by Tom Barker

Published by O'Reilly Media, Inc., 1005 Gravenstein Highway North, Sebastopol, CA 95472.

O'Reilly books may be purchased for educational, business, or sales promotional use. Online editions are also available for most titles (*http://safaribooksonline.com*). For more information, contact our corporate/institutional sales department: (800) 998-9938 or *corporate@oreilly.com*.

| | |
|---|---|
| **Editors:** Mary Treseler and Nick Lombardi | **Cover Designer:** Eleanor Volkhausen |
| **Production Editor:** Melanie Yarbrough | **Interior Designers:** Ron Bilodeau and Monica Kamsvaag |
| **Copyeditor:** Octal Publishing Services | |
| **Proofreader:** Jasmine Kwityn | **Illustrators:** Rebecca Demarest |
| **Indexer:** Deadline Driven Publishing | **Compositor:** Melanie Yarbrough |

November 2014: First Edition.

**Revision History for the First Edition:**

    2014-11-04        First release

See *http://oreilly.com/catalog/errata.csp?isbn=0636920033103* for release details.

978-1-491-94998-6

[TI]

# [ contents ]

# [ *Preface* ]

EVEN THOUGH RESPONSIVE DESIGN IS A FAIRLY UBIQUITOUS TERM AT THIS POINT, it is still considered mainly a frontend concern. In the minds of most developers, *responsive design* is also tightly coupled with media queries. With this book, however, I propose that responsive design is more of a philosophy rather than a technology: an ideal that can be approached from many different angles, from the traditional frontend-only approach, but also that there is enough information passed to the web server in each HTTP request to be responsive on the backend. And, in some cases, it is a better performing solution to push our responsiveness to the backend.

I originally intended to write this book because although I was seeing designers and engineers around me running with the ideas of producing responsive websites, I also saw business and product owners souring from the idea because they were keenly aware of the web performance costs even when we weren't always. By focusing only on the responsiveness of the client side and not looking for more performant options, we were slowly disillusioning our stakeholders on the benefits of responsiveness, and even our own effectiveness.

As I got under way with this book, it began to take on a life of its own. After we are paying attention to the performance of our responsive websites, how do we plan for that in our grooming sessions? If we are creating service-level agreements (SLAs) for the performance of our pages, how do we test that performance during development, in a *continual integration* environment?

I look to answer each of those questions in this book.

## INTENDED AUDIENCE

I wrote this book specifically with web developers in mind, specifically frontend-focused web developers who might not have ventured onto the backend yet. It's for this reason why I didn't rehash all of the existing frontend performance best practices for CSS that you can find anywhere else. That is also the reason I kept JavaScript as the primary language used in the book, especially NodeJS for all of the backend code samples.

With that said, there are enough introductory materials and explanatory notes that designers, technology leaders, and developers of every experience level and specialization should be able to benefit from the information within this book.

## CHAPTER DESCRIPTIONS

In Chapter 1, I use the top 50 most trafficked sites as a sample dataset to derive common design patterns and anti-patterns in use for responsive design. These patterns and anti-patterns will be guiding principles for us throughout the book. We also look at the idea of *mdot* sites, and discuss their pros and cons.

Chapter 2 presents a primer on web performance concepts, web runtime performance, as well as tools to track performance. This is intended as an introduction if you aren't already familiar with web performance concepts. It's also a good refresher on concepts that aren't talked about as frequently, such as memory consumption on the client side.

Chapter 3 explores incorporating responsiveness, specifically an SLA for specifying performance of our responsive websites, into the planning and grooming phases of our projects.

Chapter 4 looks at implementing performance-responsive concepts to the backend. We use NodeJS to write functionality that serves up a device-specific experience to the client. We also look at using third-party device libraries to give greater context of client capabilities rather than just examining the User Agent string and deriving device capabilities ourselves.

In Chapter 5, we look at frontend solutions to implement the performance design patterns that we identified in Chapter 1. We look at the picture element, and the secret attribute to only load device-specific images. We also look at the concept of lazy loading both images and whole chunks of a page based on client capabilities. Finally, we explore client-side device library APIs to determine form factor.

Chapter 6 uses PhantomJS to write automated tests to validate our performance SLAs and integrate these tests into a Jenkins continuous integration environment.

We close out the book with Chapter 7, in which we look at and evaluate the current frameworks available to build responsive web pages, using such criteria as how easy they are to use, what patterns and anti-patterns they use, what dependencies they have, and how much they add to the overall page payload. We also walk through Ripple, the server-side boilerplate framework that I open sourced based on the code examples from Chapter 4.

## NOTES

When writing any technology book, the pace of technology will always be faster than the pace at which we can write, edit, and publish to scale—though I have to say that O'Reilly does a great job of getting the content of their books in reader's hands as quickly as possible with their Early Access program. That said, the case study of the Alexa top 50 sites in the United States presented in Chapter 1 was conducted back in December of 2013, and since then, there are new sites in the Alexa list, the remaining sites have updated their pages, and several browser iterations with updated handling of resource loading and preloading have come out. The same is true for any proposed standards that I talk about; by the time you read this, they might have been updated or altered before being finalized.

That progress occurs is an inevitability; however, the ideas and concepts behind the tactical implementations are what are most important.

## ACKNOWLEDGMENTS

I want to thank my beautiful wife, Lynn, for her patience with me as I spent the majority of a year writing this book at night and over weekends. The same goes for my children—I tried to only write late at night when they were asleep, but I wasn't always successful with that, and so I appreciate their patience and understanding.

I want to thank Mary Treseler for giving the book a chance and for her feedback. I want to express my gratitude to Colleen Lobner, Nick Lombardi, Melanie Yarbrough, and Dianne Russell for help getting it over the finish line. I also want to thank Ilya Grigorik, Lara Swanson, Clarissa Peterson, and Jason Pamental; their feedback was vital to the completion of the book.

# [ 1 ]

# State of the Industry of Responsive Design

## The Problem with Responsive Design

I WAS SITTING IN A ROADMAP PLANNING SESSION WITH ONE OF MY TEAMS AND OUR PRODUCT PERSON, and we were discussing a redesign of our video section when my team lead started talking about how we were planning to make the video experience for our website responsive. We described having one page that would load our default HTML5 video player but would resize and load assets and playlists of different video types depending on what devices our users used to view the page. It was going to be beautiful, all encompassing, and open our video viewership up to a range of devices that had previously been locked out of the video experience that we offered.

Our product owner wrinkled her nose and said, "Well about that, we have somewhat of a bad taste about the idea of responsiveness after how the responsive home page turned out."

That took me by surprise. What was wrong with our responsive home page? I started doing some research.

The impression from the product team was that it was heavy and slow to load. When it was demonstrated for them on developer laptops, it looked great, but when they tried to show it on actual devices for their executives, it took a long time to load—too long.

I took a look at *waterfall charts*[1] for both the desktop and the smart-phone rendering of the home page. What I saw was something that in time I began noticing in a lot of other websites when I became aware of what to look for.

The smartphone rendering loaded all of the same assets as the desktop version, plus an additional CSS and sprite file. Figure 1-1 illustrates that this made the payload of the smartphone rendering slightly larger than the desktop version (1.2 MB versus 952 KB), and it added two additional HTTP requests.

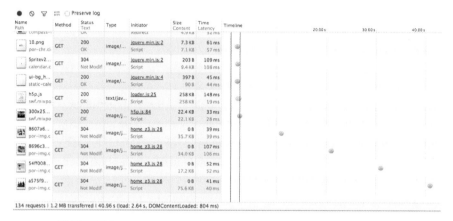

**FIGURE 1-1**

A waterfall chart of the home page, rendered for smartphone

Notice in Figure 1-1 that the total payload transferred is 1.2 MB from 134 HTTP requests. But this is the smartphone version; it should be a smaller payload. And yet it's not, as illustrated in Figure 1-2.

Observe how the total payload for the desktop is 952 KB from 132 HTTP requests. Clearly the smartphone version is loading all of the same content as the desktop version, plus an additional two files. It goes without saying that this is not responsive to the bandwidth concerns of the mobile experience.

This is completely contrary to our intention in creating a mobile page.

---

1 Waterfall charts are data visualizations that show the HTTP requests, the time it took to load the resources requested, and the payload or file size of each request that make up a web page. A much more in-depth discussion of waterfall charts concepts is presented in Chapter 2.

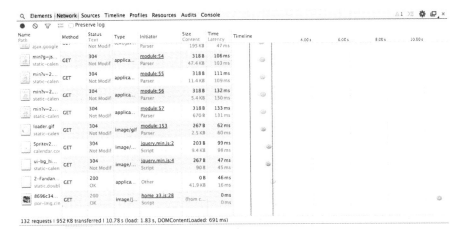

**FIGURE 1-2**

A waterfall chart of the home page rendered for desktop

And we weren't alone. I opened up a browser on my laptop and consulted HTTPWatch on my iPhone, and I went through the *Alexa.com* top 50 sites to do some competitive analysis. What I found was that 30% of the websites had a larger mobile payload than their desktop equivalent—technology companies, banks, and retailers alike.

Beyond my own research, a number of notable reports also reflected similar results. The Search Agency (a global digital marketing agency) analyzed the top 100 retail sites as well as the Fortune 100 companies' sites and produced the following reports:

- "Multichannel Retailers" (*http://bit.ly/1vqYUPh*)

- "Fortune 100 Companies" (*http://bit.ly/1r1SDlA*)

[ TIP ]

To access these reports, you will need to give The Search Agency your email address, and it will then send the reports to you.

Among its results is the chart in Figure 1-3, which shows that websites that used (or more accurately, misused) responsive design took an average of 1.91 seconds longer to load than plain, vanilla desktop websites. Most egregious of all, these same websites took 10.74 seconds longer than dedicated mobile sites.

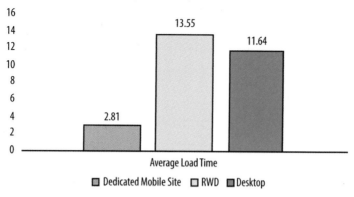

**FIGURE 1-3**

The Search Agency's comparison of average load times for responsive sites versus dedicated mobile and dedicated desktop sites

Guy Podjarny, CTO at Akamai, also wrote up a piece on his blog detailing his findings from running similar tests. He compared page sizes across a number of resolutions and found little difference between them. You can find his write-up at *http://bit.ly/1tBv6cT.*

Were we all missing the point of creating a responsive experience?

## OBSERVATIONS FROM COMPETITIVE ANALYSIS

My own observations from the Alexa list yielded some interesting data, as well. Among other things, I noticed the following:

- Of the top websites for the United States, 47% still used dedicated *mdot sites.*[2] Think about that number for a minute. These are the most trafficked websites on the Internet, arguably the leaders of their respective industries, with members including YouTube, eBay, and Target, and they are foregoing a responsive site in favor of a standalone segmented site.

---

2 An mdot site is a dedicated website created just for the mobile experience that has its own URL, usually following the convention of using "m" as a subdomain (e.g., *m.comcast.net* or *m.homedepot.com*). There are even more recent derivations of the mdot for tablets, for which "t" is a subdomain for a dedicated tablet experience (e.g., *t.homedepot.com*).

- On average, these dedicated sites were 55% smaller than respon-sive sites. The mean size of the subset that used mdots was 383 KB, whereas the responsive sites had a mean size of 851 KB (see Figure 1-4). This speaks to a gross discrepancy between intention and implementation.

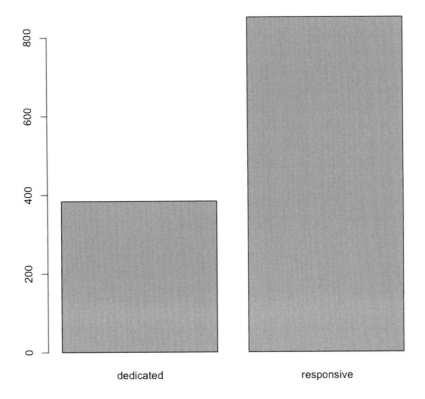

**FIGURE 1-4**
Mean file size for dedicated versus responsive websites (in KBs)

- The payload of responsive websites has a long-tailed distribution that stretches out into 4 MB, whereas mdot sites are all distrib-uted across ranges less than 1 MB. In fact, mdots are most thickly grouped into the 0 to 200 KB and 200 to 400 KB ranges. I created histograms to look at the distribution of file sizes between mdot sites and responsive sites, which you can see in Figures 1-5 and 1-6.

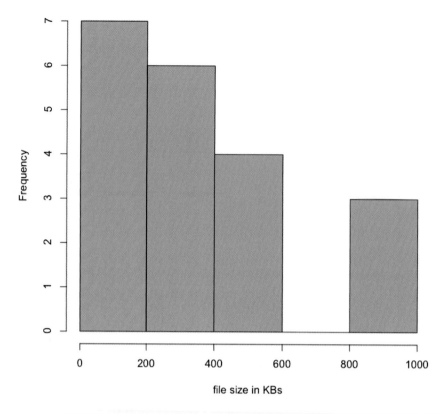

**FIGURE 1-5**
Distribution of file sizes for dedicated mobile sites (in KBs)

Note the scale of the x-axis in each histogram. The three outliers for the dedicated experiences were up against 1 MB. For the
responsive sites, 1 MB is the second largest grouping and the tail
keeps going out to 4 MB.

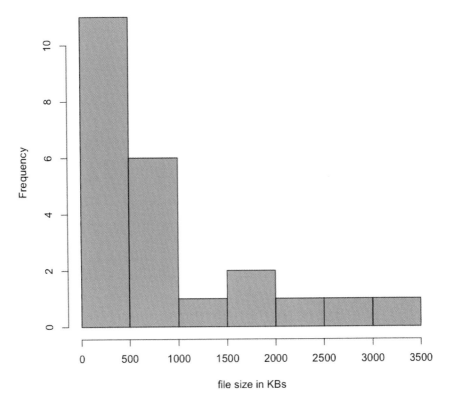

**FIGURE 1-6**
Distribution of file sizes for responsive sites (in KBs)

- Of the responsive websites, 43 percent had nearly the same or slightly more HTTP requests for their smartphone experiences compared to their desktop experiences. Contrast this to the 1.5 percent of the dedicated sites that had the same or higher HTTP requests for their smartphone experience compared to their desktop experience. Figures 1-7 and 1-8 depict this breakdown.

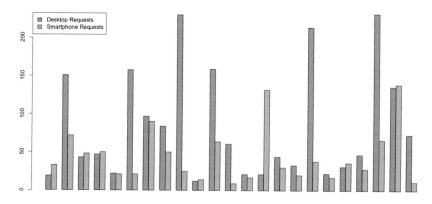

**FIGURE 1-7**

Grouped bar chart of HTTP requests for desktop and smartphone experiences on responsive sites

In Figure 1-7, notice that in each grouping, the blue bar represents the number of HTTP requests for a page served for the desktop experience, whereas the yellow bars represent the number of HTTP requests served for the same page served to a smartphone.

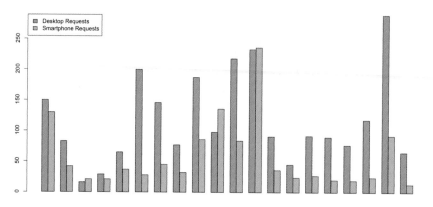

**FIGURE 1-8**

Grouped bar chart of HTTP requests for desktop and smartphone experiences on dedicated mdot sites

Again, note that for each grouping, the blue bar represents the number of HTTP requests for a page served for the desktop experience; the yellow bars show the number of HTTP requests for a smartphone.

Clearly there is an issue with how we implement responsive design. Also, there is a discernable advantage to be gained from serving a dedicated experience, at least in terms of total number of HTTP requests and total payload delivered to render a page (though it is important to note that mdots do come with their own set of problems, which we will discuss shortly). My thesis and a recurring theme that you should notice throughout this book is that responsive design and a dedicated experience are not mutually exclusive implementations but are instead aspects of the same philosophy.

In addition to the preceding metrics, I also observed a number of anti-patterns[3] and patterns that the websites which I audited seemed to follow.

## Anti-patterns

As I looked at each website on the Alexa list there were some common issues that they shared, anti-patterns that they each utilized. Let's identify and look at these anti-patterns in the following subsections.

### Load the same content for all devices

Some of the sites loaded the exact same assets for both smartphone and desktop rendering. They loaded the same CSS file across experiences, which contained media queries that handled all of the breakpoints in resolution. They loaded the same images across experiences that are just downscaled when the browser detects that the resolution warrants it.

Evidence for this offense is in the HTTP traffic. Websites that had the exact same number of HTTP requests between experiences most likely were doing this. This solution doesn't scale when we begin to talk about displays of larger resolution such as the Retina display from Apple and Ultra HD TVs.

### Load additional assets

Although loading the same set of assets for all devices ignores the intrinsic differences between devices, loading additional assets on top of the common set just for the smartphone experience is completely

---

3  Anti-patterns are commonly used solutions to problems that are inefficient, ineffective, or counterproductive. They are the opposite of design patterns, which are tested and reliable solutions to common problems.

contrary to everything we know about the mobile experience. These additional assets generally were an additional CSS file and an additional sprite file.

Websites that had more HTTP requests and a larger payload for the mobile experience than the desktop one were exhibiting this behavior. As previously noted, this was the anti-pattern that my own site was using.

### Load images at twice the size

The greatest offense was that some sites were loading an additional set of images for the smartphone version that were sized at twice the size of the desktop images. This is in addition to the regular set of images for the desktop.

The intent of loading larger images and then resizing them is that they appear sharper at the smaller size. The unfortunate side effect of this practice is that it produces websites that have mobile payloads roughly 30 percent larger than their desktop equivalents.

All of these issues had several philosophical points in common:

- They were clearly seeing the desktop version as the base upon which elements were altered or added, instead of working from the smallest version up.

- They were not exploiting the benefits or being mindful of the limitations of each platform.

- They were trying to solve the problem exclusively from the client side.

### Patterns

Not all of the sites on the Alexa list were doing it wrong—some clearly had great experiences that were optimized for the devices and resolutions that they were targeting. Let's look at some of the design patterns that they employed.

## Load device-appropriate assets

Instead of loading images twice the size of desktop images for the mobile view, some websites loaded images that were half the size of their desktop counterparts. Figures 1-9 and 1-10 show an example of this.

**FIGURE 1-9**

Loading device-specific images for the mobile experience, sized at 120 x 72 pixels and 2 KB (seen in Chrome Developer Tools)

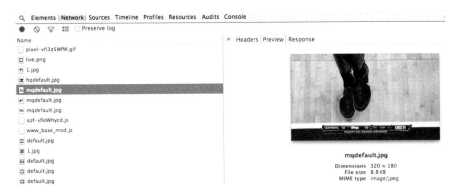

**FIGURE 1-10**

Loading device-specific images for the desktop experience, sized at 120 x 180 pixels and 8.8 KB (seen in Chrome Developer Tools)

Notice that the image in Figures 1-9 and 1-10 are the same; they're just resized to take into consideration the resources of the client environment.

In the same way, some websites loaded device-specific sprites and CSS only—not the desktop set plus additional sets for other devices. This appropriately takes into consideration the bandwidth limitations and costs of cellular networks. Unfortunately, most of the websites that on the Alexa list that did this were dedicated mdot sites. But we can utilize this pattern for responsive sites as well, as you can see in Chapter 4.

### Serve a dedicated experience from the backend

The best experiences of all were the websites that served a completely dedicated experience. Some were separate mdot sites but others had device-specific layouts and assets written to the page from the server side. This solution is sometimes called RESS (Responsive Design + Server-Side Components), but is really just combining the same logic that we used to segment traffic into an mdot site to load the appropriate content for a predefined resolution breakpoint. We discuss this solution in greater detail in Chapter 4.

For a better idea of the architecture of this solution, take a look at the sequence diagram outlining it in Figure 1-11.

Note that the websites that delivered a dedicated experience generally had the smallest payload and biggest boost to performance. This is most likely why 47 percent of the top websites still serve dedicated content.

### Lazy load dedicated experience from the frontend

Some of the sites *lazy loaded*[4] not just images but entire modules of content, both above and below the fold. In this way, they were able to avoid loading the content for each breakpoint and instead intelligently load only the content that would be necessary for the experience that is appropriate for the capabilities of the client. But instead of determining all of this at the backend, it's determined on the client side. We talk about this tactic in Chapter 5.

---

4  Lazy loading is a design pattern whereby initialization of an object or downloading of a resource is deferred until it is actually needed.

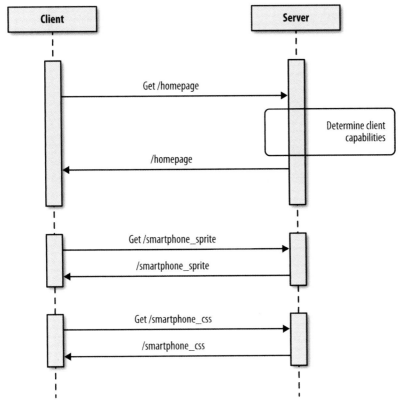

**Backend Served Dedicated Experience**

**FIGURE 1-11**

Sequence diagram serving device-appropriate experience from the backend

Figure 1-12 presents a sequence diagram detailing this approach.

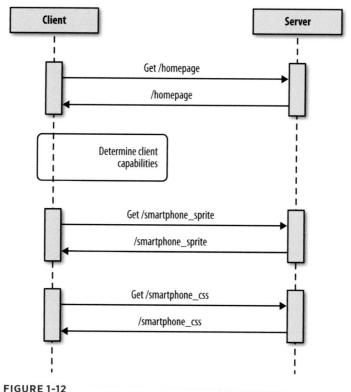

**Frontend Served Dedicated Experience**

FIGURE 1-12

Loading device-appropriate content from the client side

## HOW DID WE NOT NOTICE THIS?

I described earlier in the chapter how we demonstrated our responsive home page to our product owners. During a sprint review, we opened the page on one of our laptops, projected our desktop to a screen, and resized our browser window to reflect the different breakpoints. Although it was fun to watch the page reflow and resize on the fly, it completely missed the point of responding to different devices.

We displayed it the same way that we developed it, on a Macbook Pro using the corporate network. Of course, the performance looked fine to us. We weren't working off of a predetermined performance agreement (i.e., a service-level agreement, or SLA).[5] We weren't using an actual mobile device on a cellular network. At the time, we hadn't even acquired any devices for testing, outside of our own personal ones.

Most important, we also were not working against a performance SLA. Parity with our existing home page was an acceptable target and didn't set off any red flags in our existing performance monitors. We talk at length about this problem in Chapter 3.

## HOW DID WE GET HERE?

In the long ago days of 2008 or thereabouts, before responsive design, we would maintain two URLs: *mysite.com* and of course *m.mysite.com* (our mdot site). Each website could be different pages in the same web app, or could even be different apps, possibly even maintained by different teams of people. But this would have been the case only if we were really forward thinking and even had mobile sites to begin with, which at the time was somewhat rare.

Then, in 2011, *The Boston Globe* website relaunched, and the terms *responsive design* and *progressive enhancement* became the topic of every blog post and brainstorming session. We all read the articles coming out about how to create sites that are responsive to the capabilities of the user's device, and we all played with these concepts and became enamored with the idea. There were curmudgeons who remembered creating fluid layouts with relative heights and widths back in the early 2000s; they didn't see the difference at first, but after seeing how font sizes and images could be scaled as well, even they were turned on to the idea.

Books were written, speaking engagements were arranged, and everyone started making responsive websites. We all began talking about and using media queries to encapsulate the styles for different screen sizes. And we experimented with different ways to scale our images.

---

5   SLAs define the terms of a service contract. This definition can be as formal or informal as needed. It could apply to an application programming interface (API) provider agreeing that their API will maintain a certain amount of uptime and respond in a predetermined amount of time. It could also apply to an engineering or product team agreeing that they will fix bugs discovered in their product in a certain amount of time.

When the time came to try out these new ideas in the office "for real," we all knew that we should be starting with the smallest screen first and progressively enhance based on that. In reality, however, stakeholders wanted to see the "complete" version (i.e., the desktop version) of what they would be showing to their executives, so the design teams prioritized that work, and we all ended up building those versions first. But we could craft media queries to hold the CSS for the breakpoints and degrade the visual experience from there, so it all seemed to work out, right?

Our base CSS and JavaScript files ended up being the desktop versions (in all likelihood several hundred kilobytes in size), and we would layer on the smartphone and tablet CSS and JavaScript files after we determined client capabilities on the frontend. After that was complete, we could demonstrate the projects for stakeholders, they would demonstrate for their executives, and the project would go to production. Inevitably, one or two developers would bring up that we really should think about refactoring, because our base CSS is the desktop CSS, and oh yeah, all of our links connected out to desktop versions anyway. Yet, there was never any appetite to refactor, because the project worked, and there was no time anyway given that the next project would be starting soon, for which we needed all hands on deck to groom.

The project worked, but the problem was that we were all looking only at the frontend. Media queries and scaling images looked cool, but focusing only on those intrinsically missed the point of tailoring the holistic experience for the device that the user is currently using. It was the appearance of responsiveness without really being responsive.

We didn't just focus on how the frontend appeared; we also put all of our logic on the frontend. Relying solely on media queries to handle different device resolutions, or capability testing in JavaScript on the frontend, meant that we were already downloading unnecessary assets to the client side. This is the behavior that led to the anti-patterns that we have already identified. Figure 1-13 shows a sequence diagram that exhibits all of the anti-patterns that we identified earlier.

Differences between devices, including network infrastructure, processing power, battery life, and on-board memory, are ignored when we focus only on the frontend or only on how the page looks. In reality, these are all factors that you would need to include in any response. They are the reasons why a good percentage of the major players on the Web are still maintaining dedicated mdot sites.

**Frontend Served Dedicated Experience**

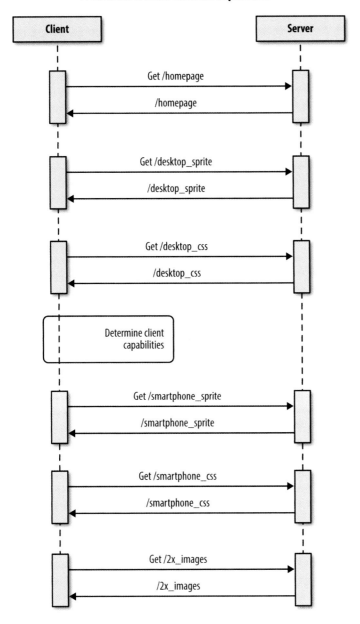

**FIGURE 1-13**

A sequence diagram of anti-patterns

## WHY NOT USE AN MDOT?

With all this talk about the benefits of mdot sites, you might be wondering why I'm not instead writing about why we all should start using them, instead. Make no mistake; I'm not endorsing mdots. Although they do have a performance advantage over how people are currently using responsive design, they have several downsides.

### Resource overhead

When I created my first mdot website in the early 2000s, I had to staff an entire new team of engineers to create and maintain it. This was mainly because our product team did not want to sacrifice the velocity on the main site to set up this mobile experience. It was also because mobile sites were—and still can be—extremely laborious endeavors because they support not just the mainstream iOS and Android devices, but an enormous array of feature phones which have different screen sizes and capabilities, including lack of JavaScript, or even support of only a subset of JavaScript functionality.

Even if you don't maintain a separate team, you would still need to track work for the mdot website as a separate body of work from your main site work; in fact, some features might not even be possible on certain feature phones.

### Segmented source code

Maintaining a separate website most likely means that you need to maintain a separate web app and separate code base. Maintaining parity between code bases is an age-old problem, solved mainly through vigilance and supervision, which means that eventually it will succumb to entropy and get out of sync. When the code bases fall out of sync, the experiences will differ between websites, and more effort will be needed to update in the future.

### Segmented URL

Having a separate mdot website means creating and maintaining a separate URL. This is contrary to the entire idea of URLs being a single location for a resource. An mdot is a second location for your site. Moreover, where is the line drawn for what goes to the mdot site? Do you set it at feature phones? Smartphones? Do tablets go as well? And what about phablets? Do they all go to the same mdot website, or do you maintain separate sites based on screen size and capability? You see how this segmentation can quickly become cumbersome.

## Pointless redirects

Having physically separate URLs also means adding in a redirect for the client to step through. Adding a redirect technically adds unneeded latency to your experience because the server has to respond back to the client with a 302 or a 304 status code, and the client must then make an additional request for the new location, as is illustrated in Figure 1-14.

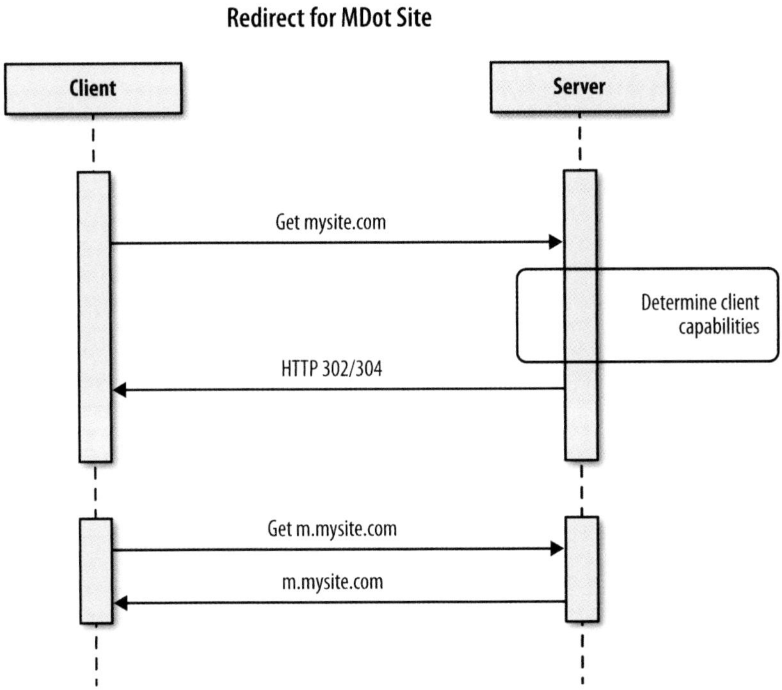

### Redirect for MDot Site

**FIGURE 1-14**
Separate URLs for a mobile site introduce HTTP redirects

## THIS MATTERS BECAUSE OF SCALE

So far, we have been talking mainly about the smartphone and desktop experience, because those, along with tablets, are the main devices that people are thinking about right now. But the industry is constantly changing and growing, and the past few years have seen a number of new devices with their own resolutions, network infrastructure, and sets of client-side assets to include.

For example, when Apple's new Retina display came out, we had to work with the design team to create unique images to include that would look great on devices using that display. This trend will continue as web development begins to show up on television guides and apps, and television displays continue to increase with 4K and 8K Ultra HDTVs.

As Google Glass becomes more pervasive, we will need to think about what the Glass experience for our websites will be. Right now, Google provides an API called the Mirror API and makes available client-side libraries to interact with the Mirror API (*http://bit.ly/1rXkSpb*).

These are just some of the new form factors that are on the leading edge. There are many more beyond that.

If we continue treating responsive design as a frontend tool, we will see the problem of bloated pages just continue to grow worse. Or we will see more companies going back to mdot sites.

## Summary

The industry is slowly turning against responsive design. Almost half of the sites that I audited are using dedicated experiences—the same solutions that we came up with in the early 2000s—instead of providing responsive sites.

Responsive design is not a flawed methodology; it is only when it is misused and treated as an add-on instead of an overarching philosophy that it can result in a bloated and counterintuitive experience. Likewise, it is only when we focus on a single aspect of responsiveness, specifically the frontend, that we lose sight of the performance of our responsive sites. Yet, performance is an aspect of responsiveness and needs to be part of the conversation, starting in planning and design. It needs to be baked into how we architect our solutions.

We have identified some design patterns in this chapter to build performance into responsiveness. We will explore these patterns, and more, in the coming chapters.

If we don't do this and build performance into our responsive solutions, the problem will only worsen as new products and devices with greater and greater resolutions are introduced along with new form factors that will require unique client interactions.

# [ 2 ]

# Primer on Performance of Web Applications

## The Basics of Measuring Performance

IF YOU ARE READING THIS BOOK, the chances are good that you have an idea of what performance is, or at the very least, you have had some discussion around the performance of your web applications. But before we go any further, let's make sure we are on the same page with respect to terminology.

If this is your first time hearing the term *web performance optimization*, quickly go pick up a copy of Steve Souders's books *High Performance Web Sites* and *Even Faster Web Sites* (both from O'Reilly). These are the standards in web performance, and they represent the base level of knowledge that all web developers should have.

The goal of this chapter is not to cover every nuance of performance. There is an enormous corpus of work that already achieves that goal, starting with the aforementioned publications of Steve Souders. Rather, the goal of this chapter is to give an overview of performance, both web performance and web runtime performance, including some of the tools used to measure performance. This way, when we reference these concepts in later chapters, there should be no confusion or ambiguity.

When talking about the performance of websites and web applications, we are speaking either of web performance or runtime performance. We define web performance as a measurement of the time from when an end user requests a piece of content to when that content is available on the user's device. We define runtime performance as an indication of how responsive your application is to user input at runtime.[1]

---

1  Runtime is when an application is running or executing.

Being aware of, quantifying, and crafting standards around the performance of your web applications is a critical aspect of application ownership. Both web performance and runtime performance have indicators that you can empirically measure and quantify. In this chapter, we will be looking at these indicators and the tools that you can use to quantify them.

[ NOTE ]

Performance indicators are measurable objectives that organizations use to define success or failure of an endeavor. They are sometimes called key performance indicators, or KPIs for short.

The types of performance indicators that we will be talking about in this chapter are as follows:

*Quantitative indicator*
An objective that can be measured empirically (think quantity of something)

*Qualitative indicator*
An objective that cannot be measured empirically (think quality of something)

*Leading indicator*
Used to predict outcomes

*Input indicator*
Used to measure resources consumed during a process

## WHAT IS WEB PERFORMANCE?

Think about each time you've surfed the Web. You open a browser, type in a URL and wait for the page to load. The time it takes from when you press Enter after typing the URL (or clicking a bookmark from your bookmark list, or clicking a link on a page) until the page renders is the web performance of the page you are visiting. If a site is performing properly, this time should not even be noticeable.

The quantitative indicators of web performance are numerous enough to list:

- Page load time

- Page file size

- Number of HTTP requests

- Page render time

The qualitative indicator of web performance can be summed up much more succinctly: perception of speed.

Before we look at these indicators, let's first discuss how pages make it to the browser and are presented to our users. When you request a web page by using a browser, the browser creates a thread to handle the request and initiates a Domain Name System (DNS) lookup at a remote DNS server, which provides the browser with the IP address for the URL you entered.

Next, the browser negotiates a Transmission Control Protocol (TCP) three-way handshake with the remote web server to establish a Transmission Control Protocol/Internet Protocol (TCP/IP) connection. This handshake consists of synchronize (SYN), synchronize-acknowledge (SYN-ACK), and acknowledge (ACK) messages that are passed between the browser and the remote server.

After the TCP connection has been established, the browser sends an HTTP GET request over the connection to the web server. The web server finds the resource and returns it in an HTTP response, the status of which is 200 to indicate a good response. If the server cannot find the resource or generates an error when trying to interpret it, or if it is redirected, the status of the HTTP response will reflect these as well. You can find the full list of status codes at *http://bit.ly/stat-codes*. Following are the most common of them:

- 200 indicates a successful response from the server

- 301 signifies a permanent redirection

- 302 indicates a temporary redirection

- 403 is a forbidden request

- 404 means that the server could not find the resource requested

- 500 denotes an error when trying to fulfill the request

- 503 specifies the service is unavailable

- 504 designates a gateway timeout

Figure 2-1 presents a sequence diagram of this transaction.

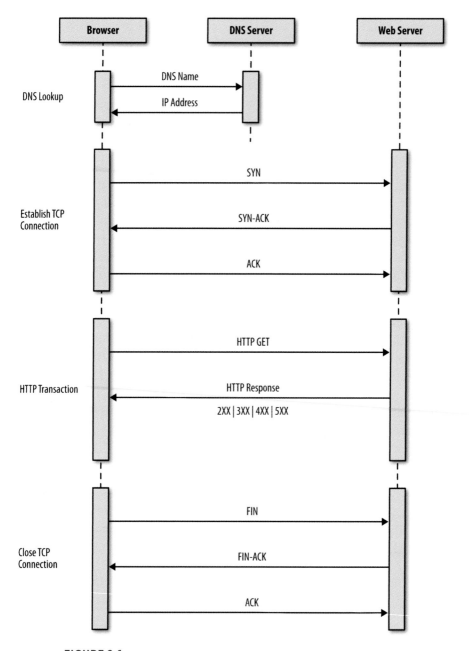

**FIGURE 2-1**

The negotiation process between a browser and web server

Keep in mind that not only is one of these transactions necessary to serve up a single HTML page, but your browser needs to make an HTTP request for each asset to which the page links—all of the images, linked CSS and JavaScript files, and any other type of external asset. (Note, however, that the browser can reuse the TCP connection for each subsequent HTTP request as long as it is connecting to the same origin.)

When the browser has the HTML for the page, it begins to parse and render the content.

The browser uses its *rendering engine* to parse and render the content. Modern browser architecture consists of several interacting modules:

*The UI layer*

This draws the interface or GUI for the browser. These are items such as the location bar, the refresh button, and other elements of the user interface (UI) that is native to the browser.

*The network layer*

This layer handles network connections, which entails tasks such as establishing TCP connections and handling the HTTP round trips. The network layer handles downloading the content and passing it to the rendering engine.

*The rendering engine*

Rendering engines are responsible for painting the content to the screen. Browser makers brand and license out their render and JavaScript engines, so you've probably heard the product names for the more popular render engines already. Arguably the most popular render engine is WebKit, which is used in Chrome (as a fork named Blink), Safari, and Opera, among many others. When the Render engine encounters JavaScript, it hands it off to the JavaScript interpreter.

*The JavaScript engine*

This handles parsing and execution of JavaScript. Just like the render engine, browser makers brand their JavaScript engines for licensing, and you most likely have heard of them. One popular JavaScript engine is Google's V8, which is used in Chrome, Chromium, and as the engine that powers Node.js.

You can see a representation of this architecture in Figure 2-2.

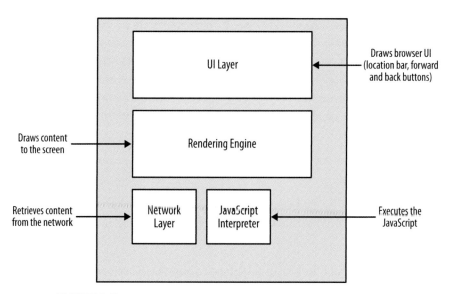

**FIGURE 2-2**

Modern browser architecture split into module components

Picture a use case in which a user types a URL into the location bar of the browser. The UI layer passes this request to the network layer, which then establishes the connection and downloads the initial page. As the packets containing chunks of HTML arrive, they are passed to the render engine. The render engine assembles the HTML as raw text and begins to perform lexical analysis—or parsing—of the characters in the text. The characters are compared to a rule set—the document type definition (DTD) that we specify in our HTML document—and converted to tokens based on the rule set. The DTD specifies the tags that make up the version of the language that we will use. The tokens are just the characters broken into meaningful segments.

Here's an example of how the network layer might return the following string:

```
<!DOCTYPE html><html><head><meta charset="UTF-8"/>
```

This string would be tokenized into meaningful chunks:

```
<!DOCTYPE html>
<html>
<head>
<meta charset="UTF-8"/>
```

The render engine then takes the tokens and converts them to Document Object Model (DOM) elements (the DOM is the in-memory representation of the page elements, and the API that JavaScript uses to access page elements). The DOM elements are laid out in a *render tree* over which the render engine then iterates. In the first iteration, the render engine lays out the positioning of the DOM elements; in the next iteration, it paints them to the screen.

If the render layer identifies a script tag during the parsing and tokenization phase, it pauses and evaluates what to do next. If the script tag points to an external JavaScript file, parsing is paused, and the network layer is engaged to download this file prior to initializing the JavaScript engine to interpret and execute the JavaScript. If the script tag contains inline JavaScript, the rendering is paused, the JavaScript engine is initialized, and the JavaScript is interpreted and executed. When execution is complete, parsing resumes.

This is an important nuance that impacts not just when DOM elements are available to JavaScript (our code might be trying to access an element on the page that has not yet been parsed and tokenized, let alone rendered), but also performance. For example, do we want to block the parsing of the page until this code is downloaded and run, or can the page be functional if we show the content first and then load the page?

Figure 2-3 illustrates this workflow for you.

Understanding how content is delivered to the browser is vital to understanding the factors that impact web performance. Also note that as a result of the rapid release schedule of browser updates, this workflow is sometimes tweaked and optimized and even changed by the browser makers.

Now that we understand the architecture of how content is delivered and presented, let's look at our performance indicators in the context of this delivery workflow.

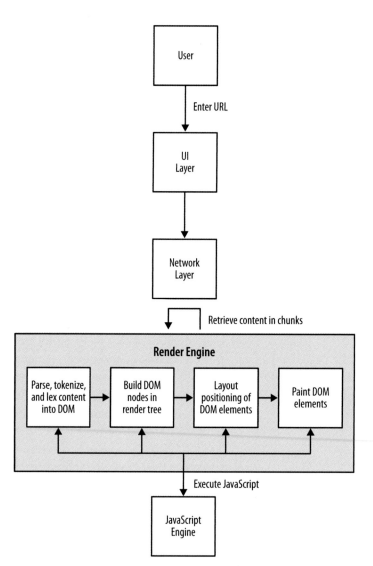

**FIGURE 2-3**

A workflow describing the loading and rendering of content in the browser

### Number of HTTP requests

Keep in mind that the browser creates an HTTP request when it gets the HTML page, and additional HTTP requests for every asset to which the page links. Depending on network latency, each HTTP request could add 20 to 200 milliseconds to the overall page load time (this number changes when you factor in browsers being able to parallel load assets). This is almost negligible when talking about a handful of assets, but when you're talking about 100 or more HTTP requests, this can add significant latency to your overall web performance.

It only makes sense to reduce the number of HTTP requests that your page requires. There are a number of ways developers can accomplish this, from concatenating different CSS or JavaScript files into a single file,[2] to merging all of their commonly used images into a single graphic file called a sprite.

### Page payload

One of the factors impacting web performance is the total file size of the page. The total payload includes the accumulated file sizes of the HTML, CSS, and JavaScript that comprise the page. It also includes all of the images, cookies, and any other media embedded on the page.

### Page load time

The number of HTTP requests and the overall page payload by themselves are just input, but the real KPI to focus on for web performance is page load time.

Page load time is the most obvious performance indicator and the easiest to quantify. Simply stated, it is the time it takes a browser to download and render all of the content on the page. Historically, this has been measured as the elapsed time from page request to the page's window onload event. More recently, as developers are becoming more adept at creating a usable experience before the page has finished loading, that end point has been moving in or even changing completely.

Specifically, there are certain use cases in which you could load content dynamically after the window.onload event has fired—as would be the case if, for instance, content is lazy loaded—and there are use cases in which the page can be usable and appear complete before the window.onload event has fired (such as when you can load content first, and load ads afterward). These cases skew the usefulness of tracking specific page load time against the window.onload event.

---

2 Per Ilya Grigorik's excellent book *High Performance Browser Networking* (O'Reilly), this practice, although useful in HTTP 1.1, becomes an anti-pattern in HTTP 2 and SDPY.

There are some options to circumvent this dilemma. Pat Meenan, who created and maintains WebPageTest, has included in WebPageTest a metric called Speed Index that essentially scores how quickly the page content is rendered. Some development teams are creating their own custom events to track when the parts of their page that they determine as core to the user experience are loaded.

However you choose to track it, page load (i.e., when your content is ready for user interaction) is the core performance indicator to monitor.

## Tools to Track Web Performance

The most common and useful tool to track web performance is the waterfall chart. Waterfall charts are visualizations that you can use to show all of the assets that make up a web page, all of the HTTP transactions needed to load these assets, and the time it takes for each HTTP request. All of these HTTP requests are rendered as bars, with the y-axis being the name or URL of the resource; sometimes the size of the resource and the HTTP status of the response for the resource are also shown in the y-axis. The x-axis, sometimes shown explicitly, sometimes not, portrays elapsed time.

The bars of a waterfall chart are drawn in the order in which the requests happen (see Figure 2-4), and the length of the bars indicates how long the transaction takes to complete. Sometimes, we can also see the total page load time and the total number of HTTP requests at the bottom of the waterfall chart. Part of the beauty of waterfall charts is that from the layout and overlapping of bars we can also ascertain when the loading of some resources blocks the loading of other resources.

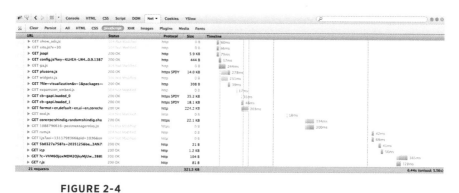

**FIGURE 2-4**

A waterfall chart generated from Firebug

These days, there are a number of different tools that can create water-fall charts for us. Some browsers provide built-in tools, such as Firebug in Firefox, or Chrome's Developer Tools. There are also free, hosted solutions such as *webpagetest.com*.

Let's take a look at some of these tools.

The simplest way to generate a waterfall chart is by using an in-browser tool. These come in several flavors, but at this point have more or less homogenized, at least in how they generate waterfall charts (some in-browser tools are far more useful than others, as we will see when we begin discussing web runtime performance).

Firebug was the first widely adopted in-browser developer tool. Available as a Firefox plug-in and first created by Joe Hewitt, Firebug set the standard by not just creating waterfall charts to show the network activity needed to load and render a page, but also to give developers access to a console to run ad hoc JavaScript and show errors, and the ability to debug and step through code in the browser.

If you aren't familiar with Firebug, you can install it by visiting *http://mzl.la/1vDXigg*. Click the "Add to Firefox" button and follow the instructions to install the add-on.

**[ NOTE ]**

Firebug is available for other browsers, but generally in a "lite" version that doesn't provide the full functionality that's available for Firefox.

**FIGURE 2-5**

The Firebug download page

To access a waterfall chart in Firebug, click the Net tab.

The industry has evolved since Firebug first came out, and now most modern web browsers come with built-in tools to measure at least some aspects of performance. Chrome comes with Developer Tools, Internet Explorer has its own developer tools, and Opera has Dragonfly.

In Chrome, to access Developer Tools, click the Chrome menu icon, select Tools, and then, click Developer Tools on the menu that opens, as demonstrated in Figure 2-6.

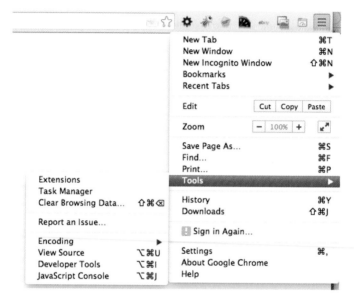

**FIGURE 2-6**
Accessing Developer Tools in Chrome

In Internet Explorer, you click Tools and then select Developer Tools.

Even mobile devices now have HTTPWatch as a native app that can run a browser within the app and show a waterfall chart for all of the resources that are loaded. HTTPWatch is available at *http://bit.ly/1rY322j*. Figures 2-7 and 2-8 give you a glimpse of HTTPWatch in action.

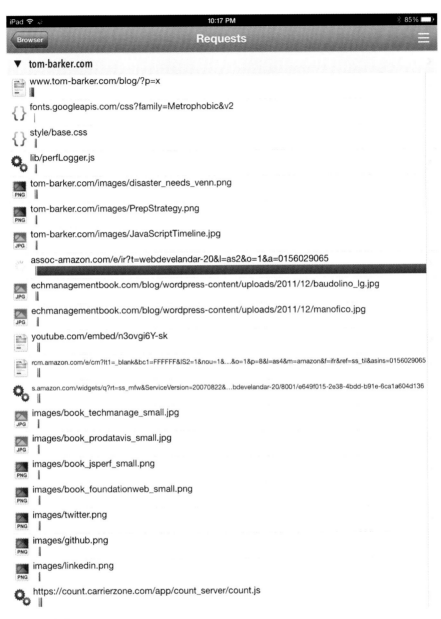

**FIGURE 2-7**
Resources loading in HTTPWatch on iOS 7

**FIGURE 2-8**

Web performance information from HTTPWatch on iOS7

In-browser tools are great for debugging, but if you want to start looking at automated solutions that can work in your *continuous integration
(CI)* environment, you need to start expanding your range of options to
include platform or headless solutions.

**[ TIP ]**

We talk at great length about headless testing and CI integration in Chapter 6.

As mentioned earlier, one of the leading platform solutions is
WebPageTest (*www.webpagetest.org*), which was created and continues
to be maintained by Pat Meenan. WebPageTest is available as a hosted
solution or open source tool that you can install and run on your network as a local copy to test behind your firewall. The code repository to
download and host is available at *http://bit.ly/1wu4Zdd*.

WebPageTest is a web application that takes a URL (and a set of config-uration parameters) as input and runs performance tests on that URL. The amount of parameters that we can configure for WebPageTest is enormous.

You can choose from a set of worldwide locations from which your tests can be run. Each location comes with one or more browsers that you can use for the test at that location. You can also specify the connection speed and the number of tests to run.

WebPageTest provides a wealth of information about the overall perfor-mance of a website, including not just waterfall charts but also charts to show the content breakdown of a given page (what percentage of the payload is made up of images, what percentage JavaScript, etc.), screen-shots to simulate the experience of how the page loads to the end user, and even CPU usage, which we will discuss in more detail later in this chapter.

Best of all, WebPageTest is fully programmable. It provides an API that you can call to provide all of this information. Figure 2-9 presents a waterfall chart generated in WebPageTest.

But when looking at web performance metrics, the ideal numbers to look at are the results from real user monitoring (sometimes called RUM) harvested from your own users. For a fully programmable solu-tion to achieve this, the World Wide Web Consortium (W3C) has stan-dardized an API that you can use to capture and report in-browser per-formance data. This is done via the Performance DOM object, an object that is native to the window object in all modern browsers.

In late 2010, the W3C created a new working group called simply the Web Performance Working Group. According to its website, the mis-sion for this working group is to provide methods to measure aspects of application performance of user agent features and APIs. What that means in a very tactical sense is that the working group has developed an API by which browsers can expose to JavaScript key web perfor-mance metrics.

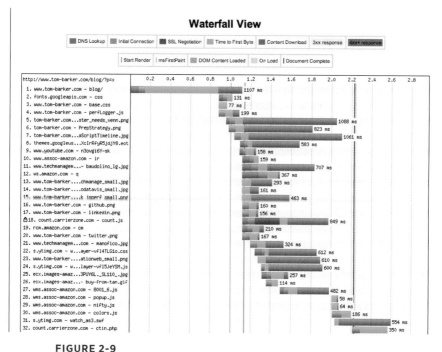

## Waterfall View

**FIGURE 2-9**

A waterfall chart generated by WebPageTest

Google's Arvind Jain and Jason Weber from Microsoft chair this working group. You can access the home page at *http://bit.ly/1t87dJ0*.

The Web Performance Working Group has created a number of new objects and events that we can use to not only quantify performance metrics, but also optimize performance. Here is a high-level overview of these objects and interfaces:

*The* performance *object*

This object exposes several objects, such as PerformanceNavigation, PerformanceTiming, MemoryInfo, as well as the capability to record high resolution time for submillisecond timing

*The Page Visibilty API*

This interface gives developers the capability to check whether a given page is visible or hidden, which makes it possible to optimize memory utilization around animations, or network resources for polling operations.

If you type `window.performance` in a JavaScript console, you will see that it returns an object of type `Performance` with several objects and methods that it exposes. As of this writing, the standard set of objects is `window.performance.timing` for type `PerformanceTiming` and `window.performance.navigation` for type `PerformanceNavigation`. Chrome supports `window.performance.memory` for type `MemoryInfo`. We will discuss the `MemoryInfo` object in the "Web Runtime Performance" section later in this chapter.

It is the `PerformanceTiming` object that is most useful for monitoring of real user metrics; see Figure 2-10 for a screenshot of the `Performance` object and the `PerformanceTiming` object in the console.

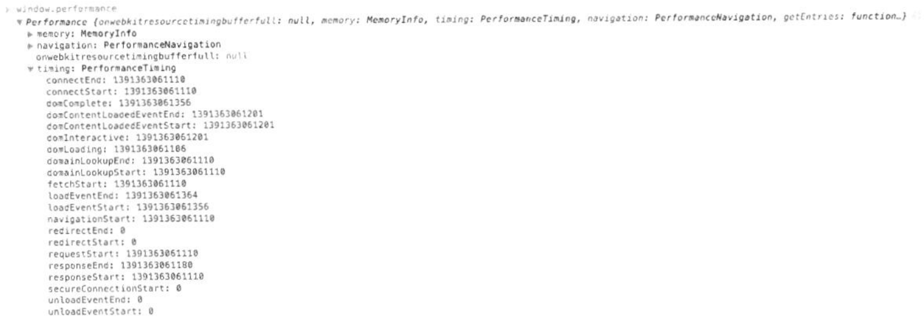

**FIGURE 2-10**

The `Performance` object viewed in the console with the `Performance.Timing` object expanded

Keep in mind that the purpose of real user monitoring is to gather actual performance metrics from real users, as opposed to synthetic performance testing, which generates artificial tests in a lab or with an agent following a prescribed script. The benefit of RUM is that you capture and analyze the real performance of your actual user base.

Table 2-1 lists the properties in the `PerformanceTiming` object.

**TABLE 2-1.** The PerformanceTiming object properties

| PROPERTY | DESCRIPTION |
|---|---|
| navigationStart | Captures when navigation begins, either when the browser starts to unload the previous page if there is one, or if not, when it begins to fetch the content. It will either contain the unloadEventStart data or the fetchStart data. If you want to track end-to-end time, you will often begin with this value. |
| unloadEventStart/unloadEventEnd | Captures when the browser begins to unload and finishes unloading the previous page (if there is a previous page at the same domain to unload). |
| domainLookupStart/domainLookupEnd | Captures when the browser begins and completes the DNS lookup for the requested content. |
| redirectStart/redirectEnd | Captures when the browser begins and completes any HTTP redirects. |
| connectStart/connectEnd | Captures when the browser begins and finishes establishing the TCP connection to the remote server for the current page. |
| fetchStart | Captures when the browser first begins to check cache for the requested resource. |
| requestStart | Captures when the browser sends the HTTP request for the requested resource. |
| responseStart/responseEnd | Captures when the browser first registers and finishes receiving the server response. |
| domLoading/domComplete | Captures when the document begins and finishes loading. |
| domContentLoadedEventEnd/ domContentLoadedEventStart | Captures when the document's DOMContentLoaded event begins and finishes loading, which corresponds to when the browser has completed loading all of the content and running all of the included scripts on the page. |
| domInteractive | Captures when the page's Document.ready State property changes to 'interactive', causing the readystatechange event to be fired. |
| loadEventEnd/loadEventStart | Captures directly before the point at which the load event is fired and right after the load event is fired. |

Figure 2-11 shows the order in which these events occur.

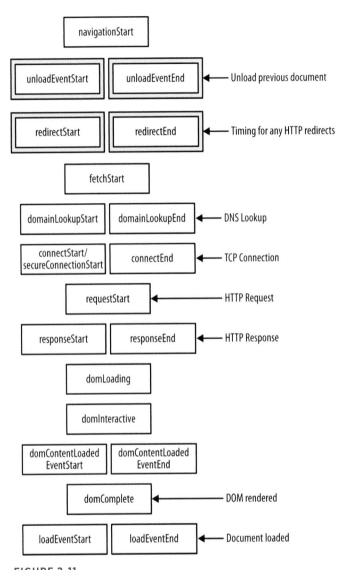

**FIGURE 2-11**
The performance timing events

You can craft your own JavaScript libraries to embed in your pages and capture actual RUM from user traffic. Essentially, the JavaScript captures these events and sends them to a server-side endpoint that you can set up to save and analyze these metrics. I have created just such a library at *https://github.com/tomjbarker/perfLogger* that you are welcome to use.

# Web Runtime Performance

As we've been discussing, web performance tracks the time it takes to deliver content to your user. Now it's time to look at *web runtime performance*, which tracks how your application behaves when the user begins interacting with it.

For traditional compiled applications, runtime performance is about *memory management, garbage collection*, and *threading*. This is because compiled applications run on the kernel and use the system's resources directly.

Running web applications on the client side is different from running compiled applications. This is because they are running in a sandbox, or to put it more specifically, the browser. When they are running, web applications use the resources of the browser. The browser, in turn, has its own footprint of pre-allocated virtual memory from the kernel in which it runs and consumes system resources. So, when we talk about web runtime performance, we are talking about how our applications are running on the client side in the browser, and making the browser perform in its own footprint in virtual memory. Figure 2-12 offers a diagram of a web app running in the browser's footprint within resident memory.

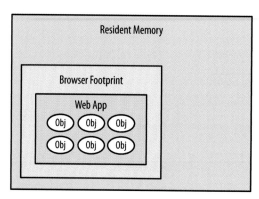

**FIGURE 2-12**

A web application running in the browser's pre-allocated footprint in resident memory

Following are some of the factors we need to consider that impact web runtime performance:

*Memory management and garbage collection*

One of the first things we need to look at is whether we are clogging up the browser's memory allocation with objects that we don't need and retaining those objects while creating even more. Do we have any mechanism to cap the creation of objects in JavaScript over time, or will the application consume more memory the more and longer it is used? Is there a memory leak?

Garbage collecting unneeded objects can cause pauses in rendering or animation that can make your user experience seem jagged. We can minimize garbage collection by reducing the amount of objects that we create and reusing objects when possible.

*Layout*

Are we updating the DOM to cause the page to be re-rendered around our updates? This is generally due to large-scale style changes that requires the render engine to recalculate sizes and locations of elements on the page.

*Expensive paints*

Are we taxing the browser by making it repaint areas as the user scrolls the page? Animating or updating any element property other than position, scale, rotation or opacity will cause the render engine to repaint that element and consume cycles. Position, scale, rotation, and opacity are the final properties of an element that the render engine configures, and so will take the least amount of rework to update these.

If we animate width, height, background, or any other property, the render engine will need to walk through layout and repaint the elements again, which will consume more cycles to render or animate. Even worse, if we cause a repaint of a parent element, the render engine will need to repaint all of the child elements, compounding the hit on runtime performance.

*Synchronous calls*

Are we blocking user action because we're waiting for a synchronous call to return? This is common when you have checkboxes or some other way to accept input and update state on the server, and wait to get confirmation that the update happened. This will make the page appear sluggish.

*CPU usage*

> How hard is the browser working to render the page and execute our client-side code?

The performance indicators that we will be looking at for web runtime performance are frames per second and CPU usage.

## FRAMES PER SECOND

Frames per second (FPS) is a familiar measurement for animators, game developers, and cinematographers. It is the rate at which a system redraws a screen. Per Paul Bakaus's excellent blog post "The Illusion of Motion" (*http://bit.ly/1ou97Zn*), the ideal frame rate for humans to perceive smooth, life-like motion is 60 FPS.

There is also a web app called Frames Per Second (*http://frames-per-second.appspot.com*) that demonstrates animations in a browser at different frame rates. It's interesting to watch the demonstration and discern how your own eyes react to the same animations at different frame rates.

FPS is also an important performance indicator for browsers because it reflects how smoothly animations run and the window scrolls. Jagged scrolling especially has become a hallmark for web runtime performance issues.

### Monitoring FPS in Google Chrome

Google is currently the leader in creating in-browser tools to track runtime performance. It has included the ability to track FPS as part of Chrome's built-in Developer Tools. To see this, click the Rendering tab and then check the "Show FPS meter" box (see Figure 2-13).

**FIGURE 2-13**

Enabling the FPS meter in Chrome Developer Tools

This renders a small time series chart at the upper right of the browser that shows the current FPS as well as how the number of frames per second have been trending, as depicted in Figure 2-14. Using this, you can explicitly track how your page performs during actual usage.

**FIGURE 2-14**
Chrome's FPS meter, in the upper-right corner of the web page

Although the FPS meter is a great tool to track your frames per second, the most useful tool, so far, to debug why you are experiencing drops in frame rate is the Timeline tool, also available in Chrome Developer Tools (see Figure 2-15).

Using the Timeline tool, you can track and analyze what the browser is doing as it runs. It offers three operating modes: Frames, Events, and Memory. Let's take a look at Frames mode.

**Frames mode**

In this mode, the Timeline tool exposes the rendering performance of your web app. Figure 2-15 presents the Frames mode screen layout.

You

can see two different panes in the Timeline tool. The top pane displays the active mode (on the lefthand side) along with a series of vertical bars that represent frames. The bottom pane is the Frames view, which presents waterfall-like horizontal bars to indicate how long a given action took within the frame. You can see a description of the action in the left margin; the actions correspond to what the browser is perform-ing. At the far right side of the Frames view is a pie chart that shows a breakdown of what actions took the most time in the given frame. The actions included are the following:

- Layout
- Paint Setup

- Paint

- Recalculate Style

- Timer Fired

- Composite Layers

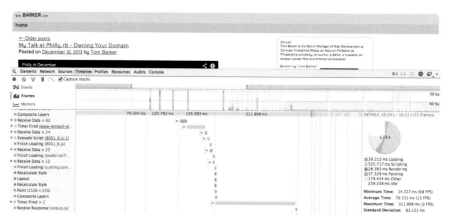

**FIGURE 2-15**

Chrome's Timeline tool in Frames mode

Figure 2-15 shows that running JavaScript took around half of the time, 525 milliseconds out the 1.02 second total.

Using the Timeline tool, in Frame mode, you can easily identify the biggest impacts on your frame rate by looking for the longest bars in the Frame view.

## MEMORY PROFILING

Memory profiling is the practice of monitoring the patterns of memory consumption that our applications use. This is useful for detecting memory leaks or the creation of objects that are never destroyed—in JavaScript, this is usually when we programmatically assign event handlers to DOM objects and forget to remove the event handlers. More nuanced than just detecting leakages, profiling is also useful for optimizing the memory usage of our applications over time. We should intelligently create, destroy, or reuse objects and always be mindful of scope to avoid profiling charts that trend upward in an ever-growing series of spikes. Figure 2-16 depicts the JavaScript heap.

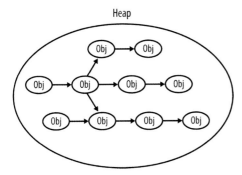

Heap

**FIGURE 2-16**
Objects in the JavaScript heap

Although the in-browser capabilities are much more robust than they have ever been, this is still an area that needs to be expanded and standardized. So far, Google has done the most to make in-browser memory management tools available to developers.

### The MemoryInfo Object

Among the memory management tools available in Chrome, the first that we will look at is the `MemoryInfo` object, which is available via the `Performance` object. The screenshot in Figure 2-17 shows a console view.

```
> window.performance
  ▼ Performance {onwebkitresourcetimingbufferfull: null, memory: MemoryInfo, timing: PerformanceTiming, navigation: PerformanceNavigation, getEntries: function…}
    ▼ memory: MemoryInfo
       jsHeapSizeLimit: 793000000
       totalJSHeapSize: 26800000
       usedJSHeapSize: 17100000
    ▶ __proto__: MemoryInfo
    ▶ navigation: PerformanceNavigation
      onwebkitresourcetimingbufferfull: null
    ▶ timing: PerformanceTiming
    ▶ __proto__: Performance
```

**FIGURE 2-17**
The MemoryInfo object

You can access the `MemoryInfo` object like so:

```
>>performance.memory
MemoryInfo {jsHeapSizeLimit: 793000000, usedJSHeapSize:
37300000, totalJSHeapSize: 56800000}
```

Table 2-2 presents the heap properties associated with `MemoryInfo`.

**TABLE 2-2.** MemoryInfo object properties

| OBJECT PROPERTY | DEFINITION |
|---|---|
| jsHeapSizeLimit | The upper boundary on the heap size |
| usedJSHeapSize | The amount of memory that all of the current objects in the heap are using |
| totalJSHeapSize | The total size of the heap including free space not used by objects |

These properties reference the availability and usage of the JavaScript heap. The heap is the collection of JavaScript objects that the interpreter keeps in resident memory. In the heap, each object is an interconnected node, connected via properties such as the prototype chain or composed objects. JavaScript running in the browser references the objects in the heap via object references. When you destroy an object in JavaScript, what you are really doing is destroying the object reference. When the interpreter sees objects in the heap with no object references, the garbage collection process removes the object from the heap.

Using the MemoryInfo object, we can pull RUM around memory consumption for our user base, or we can track these metrics in our lab to identify any potential memory issues before our code goes to production.

### The Timeline tool

In addition to offering the Frames mode for debugging a web application's frame rate, Chrome's Timeline tool also has Memory mode (shown in Figure 2-18) to visualize the memory used by your application over time and exposes the number of documents, DOM nodes, and event listeners that are held in memory.

**FIGURE 2-18**

The Chrome Timeline tool in Memory mode

The top pane shows the memory profile chart, whereas the very bottom pane shows the count of documents, nodes, and listeners. Note how the blue shaded area represents memory usage, visualizing the amount of heap space used. As more objects are created, the memory usage climbs; as those objects are destroyed and garbage collected, the memory usage falls.

You can find a great article on memory management from the Mozilla Developer Network at *http://mzl.la/1r1RzOG*.

Firefox has begun to expose memory usage as well, via an "about:memory" page, though the Firefox implementation is more of a static informational page rather than an exposed API. As such, because it can't be easily plugged into a programmatic process and generate empirical data, the about:memory page is tailored more toward Firefox users (albeit advanced users) rather than being part of a developer's toolset for runtime performance management.

To access the "about:memory" page in Firefox, in the browser's location bar, type **about:memory**. Figure 2-19 shows how the page appears.

**FIGURE 2-19**

Firefox's about:memory page

Looking at Figure 2.19, you can see the memory allocations made by the browser at the operating system level as well as heap allocations made for each page that the browser has open.

## Summary

This chapter explored web performance and web runtime performance. We looked at how content is served from a web server to a browser and the potential bottlenecks in that delivery as well as the potential bottlenecks in the rendering of that content. We also looked at performance indicators that speak to how our web applications perform during runtime, which is the other key aspect of performance: not just how fast we can deliver content to the end user but also how usable our application is after it has been delivered.

We looked at tools that quantify and track both types of performance.

Most important, we level-set expectations with respect to concepts that we will be talking about at length throughout the rest of this book. As we talk about concepts such as reducing page payload and number of HTTP requests or avoiding repainting parts of a page, you can refer back to this chapter for context.

Chapter 3 looks at how you can start building responsiveness into your overall business methodology and the software development life cycle.

# [ 3 ]

# Start with a Plan

## A Journey Down the Slippery Slope

I REMEMBER THE FIRST TIME I STARTED A PROJECT THAT HAD ASPIRA-
TIONS OF BEING *responsive*. Everyone on the team bought in: the product owner, the design group, engineering. We groomed and groomed,
exploring together what our collective ideas of what being responsive
meant. We were excited about the possibilities and giddy with the taste
of something new.

Until that point, we maintained an mdot website with a separate developer dedicated to keeping it current and aligned with the main site. In
engineering, we were looking forward to folding that developer back
into the main team, and we were enjoying the collaboration we were
experiencing with the design group.

We were a few weeks in and had nothing yet to demonstrate or even
show to the executive team, but we nonetheless glowed about what
a great learning experience we were having. Naturally, the executive
team wasn't glowing quite as brightly and wanted to have something
concrete that they could talk about with their leadership team and their
peers. A section of the design team was split off from the working team
to mock up what the website would look like on the desktop, just as a
talking point. Of course, after that mock-up was shown around, it was
approved and suddenly became the final design from which we had to
work and on which we had to base an end date.

Even though we conceptually knew that we should have started with
the mobile view first and layered on from there, we quickly deferred all
intentions to craft the small view for a later iteration and began to focus
on creating the vision of the final product. It was only a year later that
we started to craft what the experience on other devices might be, but

by then the main desktop experience had become so feature rich that it was slow going, and it became a pet project that spanned months to mock up what the responsive site could be.

By then, it was too late; the mockup had about the same page payload as the desktop version, but it performed poorly when displayed on actual devices. The site remained a desktop-only experience.

How closely does that mirror your own experiences, either with previous projects or current ones? How did it all go wrong? I thought on this for a while: what learnings could I carry out from this to benefit future projects?

At a high level, we did ourselves in. From within the team, it all appeared to be fun exploration and collaboration, feeling out the boundaries of something that was new to us. From outside the team, it looked as if we had no plan and no end goal in sight—which was true. In the long term, our lack of planning undermined the executive team's trust in the working team, and set the precedent that we needed intervention and an end goal outlined for us.

In this chapter, I outline how to craft a plan for your team so that you can quickly create deliverables that can become talking points for the leadership team, all while still sticking to the goals of having a responsive, high-performing site.

## Project Plans

Responsive projects really are no different from any other project, in so much as they generally will benefit from having a project plan. In program and project management literature, there are several flavors of project plans, depending on methodology, organization, business sector, and whom you ask (among other factors), but in general, project plans will consist of the following steps:

1. Assess/summarize the overall task

2. Establish rough milestones and timelines

3. List dependencies and risks

4. List key performance indicators (KPIs) that measure success

The only difference with a responsive project is that requirements which speak to the various device experiences should be explicit in each of the aforementioned steps. Let's look at each of these steps in greater detail.

## ASSESSING AND SUMMARIZING THE OVERALL TASK

Assessing the overall task involves collecting requirements and determining the content strategy for your project. This could mean having a discussion with your stakeholders or product manager to establish the philosophy or vision of your site and the intended use cases that you are developing for. This could also mean working with them to do extensive user testing and competitive analysis to determine the content strategy.

Part of assessing the task is to answer certain relevant questions. For example, are you trying to re-create the viewing experience of a 10-foot video screen, or are you trying to serve textual content? Are you creating a companion experience to a television product, or are you crafting an intranet experience available to a locked-down set of users.

Does your project even need to be responsive? A number of years ago I worked on a web app project that aimed to assist construction managers in identifying obvious hazards such as upturned dirt that was not surrounded by silt fences. By the very nature of this single use case, the project never needed a desktop experience, so we built for the smartphone dimensions and just let the size of the page naturally scale up for desktop experiences (there were no tablets back then).

The use cases and overall project vision should explicitly answer the question: what are the viewports that I am targeting for this project? These viewports should be part of your requirements, and as we progress through each step in the project plan, we will refer back to them, but again the very first step is to identify which ones we are explicitly targeting. Figure 3-1 depicts a sampling of potential viewports that you might target as well as their relative size differences.

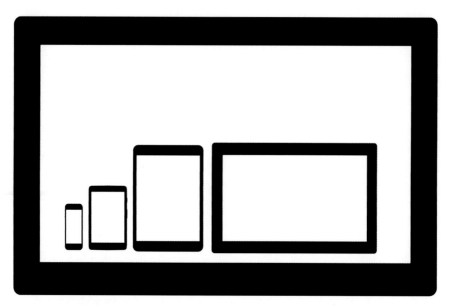

**FIGURE 3-1**

A sample of viewports ranging from smartphones, tablets, laptops, and HDTVs, covering differences not only in size, but also orientation

Beyond just the difference in size, you also need to consider the difference in viewing distance, battery life, and network speed and reliability for each device experience.

Studies have revealed that the average distance from a user's face to the screen for smartphones is only 12.6 inches.[1] Compare this to an average of 25 inches for laptops,[2] and 96 inches for televisions.[3] (See Figure 3-2.)

---

1  *http://bit.ly/1upRIDu*

2  *http://bit.ly/10pmjDm*

3  *http://bit.ly/1x32EG6*

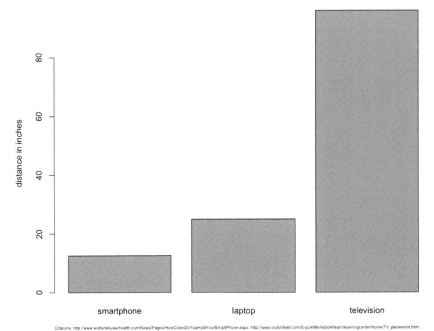

Average Viewing Distance by Device

Citations: http://www.wolterskluwerhealth.com/News/Pages/HowCloseDoYouHoldYourSmartPhone.aspx, http://www.crutchfield.com/S-yLHM6v9a5pH/learn/learningcenter/home/TV_placement.html, http://www.wave-fcm.com/Attachments/5_Laptop_Notebook_Computers_and_Ergonomics.pdf

**FIGURE 3-2**

Average viewing distance by device, in inches

These variations in viewing distances mean differences in, among other things, image and font sizes, each of which require different CSS rules and potentially different images for each experience. You need to account for these when assessing the size of the overall tasks.

Average network speeds are equally staggered across mediums. According to Akamai's 2013 report "State of the Internet" (*http://bit. ly/1tDGysM*), the average broadband connection speed in the United States was 11.6 megabits per second (Mbps), whereas the average mobile connection speed was 5.3 Mbps. See Figure 3-3.

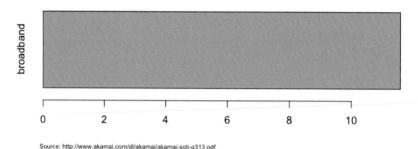
**Average Connection Speeds (in Mbps) in the US**

speed in Mbps

mobile

broadband

0    2    4    6    8    10

Source: http://www.akamai.com/dl/akamai/akamai-soti-q313.pdf

**FIGURE 3-3**
Average connection speeds (Mbps) in the United States in 2013

This discrepancy in connection speed obviously speaks to the issue of how long it will take to deliver and render content to a device. This means that you need to plan your feature set and your performance budget accordingly.

### Establishing rough milestones and timelines

Don't plan in a vacuum; after you have established the target viewports, you should perform competitive analysis. Make the effort to research internal and external applications that serve similar functions and come up with a performance baseline for each device experience based on this competitive analysis. Intelligently plot out what the current landscape is for performance and make an intentional decision of where in that landscape you want your application to be.

Figure 3-4 presents the results of a theoretical competitive analysis of page load times for mobile experiences. In this theoretical data set, we can see that the majority of our internal and external competitors fall in the 500-millisecond to 1-second range. Is that an acceptable range for our web application, or do we want to be performance leaders and aim for the sub–500-millisecond tier? What sort of features do the sites in that range have, and are we OK paring down our feature set to get our page load times that low?

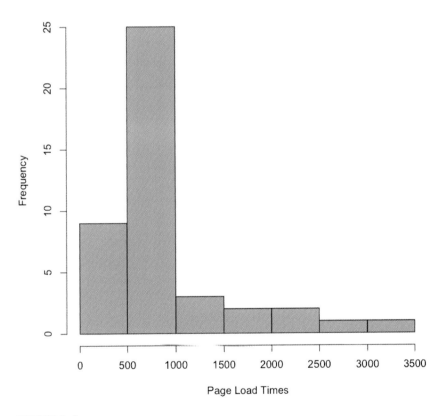

**FIGURE 3-4**

Histogram of result from theoretical analysis of competitor page load times

In Figure 3-4, note the outliers that take up to 3.5 seconds. This decision—this line in the sand—is where you are intentionally positioning your application in the performance baseline. This is your performance service-level agreement.

### Determining a performance service-level agreement

A service-level agreement (SLA) is a commitment of quality from a service provider, traditionally stipulating aspects such as response times, up times, and error rates. As owners of a website, that site is a service we are providing and we should feel compelled to provide an SLA to our end users as well as internal stakeholders for how our website performs.

Your performance SLA should be explicit both in what it is stating and in how it will be measured. A good performance SLA might read as follows:

> For the 95th percentile, the page load times of our website will be 1 second or less on a small screen experience, and 3 seconds or less on a large screen experience, measured via synthetic testing.

When you determine your performance SLA, this decision should influence what features you put on each experience and how you show them. You should also publish this SLA in your documentation to make it available to your team and stakeholders.

### CRAFTING ROUGH MILESTONES AND TIMELINES

Now that you have an understanding based not only on what the product request is, but also of what it would really involve from a performance perspective, you can begin to flesh out its implementation. This can be as rich and complex as a hierarchical tree structure of user stories, to as high level as a spreadsheet of T-shirt sized steps.[4]

But all of your device/resolution/viewport–specific states are explicitly called out and accounted for as milestones in the overall timeline, as illustrated in Figure 3-5.

---

4  T-shirt sizing is a way to practice agile estimating. Estimates are bucketed in small-, medium-, or large-sized efforts, relative to each other. Rally has a write-up on the practice here: *http://bit.ly/1w02oGt*.

| User Story | Risks | Dependencies | T-Shirt Size |
|---|---|---|---|
| Create environments | | | 1 sprint |
| Identify Endpoints | | | 1 sprint |
| Create 1024 × 768 view of homepage (for older laptops and Ipad 1 and 2s) | | | 1 sprint |
| Create 2048 × 1536 view of homepage (for Ipad 3 and up) | | | 1 sprint |
| Create 768 × 1024 view of homepage (for iPad minis) | | | 1 sprint |
| Create 2560 × 1440 view of homepage (for laptops) | | | 1 sprint |
| Create 640 × 1136 view of homepage (for iPhone 5s) | | | 1 sprint |

**FIGURE 3-5**

A sample of high-level plan with milestones built in for each resolution and device targeted

To be clear, the high-level stories that we are indicating in Figure 3-5 (Create 1024 × 768 view, Create 2560 ×1440 view) are not assuming that these are distinct pages or anything of the sort—this is just a collection of milestones that will be accomplished (objectives, if you will); the tactics of how to accomplish that are not implied.

[ NOTE ]

Radu Chelariu wrote a great article for *Smashing Magazine* that outlines a broad swath of resolutions by device. You can read it at *http://bit.ly/ZqcGUb.*

Oh, one more thing: because we have committed to adhering to a performance SLA, we should be sure to include high-level stories that define the setup of the infrastructure and process for monitoring our SLA. Let's add these supporting stories to our existing list, as shown in Figure 3-6.

| User Story | Risks | Dependencies | T-Shirt Size |
|---|---|---|---|
| Create environments | | | 1 sprint |
| Identify Endpoints | | | 1 sprint |
| Create 1024 × 768 view of homepage (for older laptops and Ipad 1 and 2s) | | | 1 sprint |
| Create 2048 × 1536 view of homepage (for Ipad 3 and up) | | | 1 sprint |
| Create 768 × 1024 view of homepage (for iPad minis) | | | 1 sprint |
| Create 2560 × 1440 view of homepage (for laptops) | | | 1 sprint |
| Create 640 × 1136 view of homepage (for iPhone 5s) | | | 1 sprint |
| Create environments for internal WebPageTest instance | | | 1 sprint |
| Set up and configure internal WebPageTest instance | | | 1 sprint |
| Integrate SLA check into CI workflow | | | 1 sprint |

**FIGURE 3-6**

Our high-level story list, updated to account for tracking our SLA

## LIST DEPENDENCIES AND RISKS

After we have the high-level stories mapped out with time estimates for each one, we can begin to flesh out the risks and dependencies for each story. These should be fairly straightforward and commonsensical, but you still need to call them out both to properly account for the steps needed to accomplish the stories and to show your stakeholders that those steps are being taken. Figure 3-7 is a continuation of the previous example, this time fleshed out with dependencies and risks.

Figure 3-7 illustrates how we can see that the dependencies have the designs or wireframes, have environments set up, and have a defined performance SLA. By calling these out explicitly, we can see what stories need to be predicated by other stories. It also makes it possible for us to craft a meaningful timeline by staggering these stories.

| User Story | Risks | Dependencies | T-Shirt Size |
|---|---|---|---|
| Create environments | | Infrastructure | 1 sprint |
| Identify Endpoints | | API Team, Connectivity to API endpoints | 1 sprint |
| Create 1024 × 768 view of homepage (for older laptops and Ipad 1 and 2s) | Must adhere to SLA for tablets | Need designs or wireframes for this resolution, need SLA for this device | 1 sprint |
| Create 2048 × 1536 view of homepage (for Ipad 3 and up) | Must adhere to SLA for tablets | Need designs or wireframes for this resolution, need SLA for this device | 1 sprint |
| Create 768 × 1024 view of homepage (for iPad minis) | Must adhere to SLA for tablets | Need designs or wireframes for this resolution, need SLA for this device | 1 sprint |
| Create 2560 × 1440 view of homepage (for laptops) | Must adhere to SLA laptop/desktop | Need designs or wireframes for this resolution, need SLA for this device | 1 sprint |
| Create 640 × 1136 view of homepage (for iPhone 5s) | Must adhere to SLA for smartphones | Need designs or wireframes for this resolution, need SLA for this device | 1 sprint |
| Create environments for internal WebPageTest instance | | Infrastructure | 1 sprint |
| Set up and configure internal WebPageTest instance | | need environments set up | 1 sprint |
| Integrate SLA check into CI workflow | | | 1 sprint |

FIGURE 3-7

Dependencies and risks outlined in the overall project story plan

## Crafting timelines

Now that we know the steps that will be involved in completing the task, we can construct very rough timelines. By using high-level T-shirt sizes for each task we can group them in a meaningful manner and lay them horizontally across a timeline.

For this example, let's assume that we have two-week iterations. Assuming that we know our team's velocity, we can construct a very rough *swag* of what would fit in each iteration. We can group all of the research and set up stories into a single iteration. Then we can group a handful of stories into another iteration, and the remainder of the stories into a third iteration.

With the following methodology, we can see that the task is probably at least a six-week project, if not longer, as demonstrated in Figure 3-8.

| Week 1 | Week 2 | Week 3 | Week 4 |
|---|---|---|---|
| Sprint A | | Sprint B | |
| Create environments | | Create 640 × 1136 view of homepage (for iPhone 5s) | |
| Identify Endpoints | | Create 768 × 1024 view of homepage (for iPad minis) | |
| Create environments for internal WebPageTest instance | | Create 1024 × 768 view of homepage (for older laptops and Ipad 1 and 2s) | |
| Set up and configure internal WebPageTest instance | | Integrate SLA check into CI workflow | |

| Week 5 | Week 6 | Week 7 | Week 8 |
|---|---|---|---|
| Sprint C | | | |
| Create 2048 × 1536  view of homepage (for Ipad 3 and up) | | | |
| Create 2560 × 1440  view of homepage (for laptops) | | | |

**FIGURE 3-8**

Our high-level stories laid out across very rough timelines

The important thing to note here is that these are very rough timelines. A moment ago, I intentionally used the word "swag," which stands for Scientific Wild-Ass Guess. In slightly more polite society, it's sometimes called a guesstimate, or back of the napkin calculation. As long as you are clear with your stakeholders that this timeline is subject to change as you find out more information, and you continue to communicate as new developments arise, you should be good.

## KPIs THAT MEASURE SUCCESS

We have so far assessed the task, created rough timelines around it, and listed dependencies involved in achieving those timelines. Next, we need to ensure that we have clearly defined criteria for success. In truth, the KPIs that measure the success of the project should already exist before our product or business team come to us with the ask, but we need to work with them to ensure that first these KPIs are visible and obvious to the entire team, and second that our solution to the ask actually is aligned to satisfy the intended criteria.

If KPIs are not determined at this point, we need to collaborate with our stakeholders to establish them. How else will we know if our project is a success, and how else will we be able to iterate to improve on those results?

**KEEP TO YOUR PERFORMANCE SLA**

We now have a plan of what we need to get done, we have identified milestones, and we are communicating when we will have each milestone complete. We have a performance SLA for each experience; we are ready to start the work.

But during development it is imperative to stick to our performance SLA. You need to ensure that performance testing is a part of your continuous integration workflow and that you have alerts go off when you violate your SLA. We talk at length about how to do this in Chapter 6.

Use your SLA as a discussion point when evaluating new features. Will these new features impact your performance? Will slight alterations in the business rule result in a higher-performing product?

## Summary

The purpose of this chapter was not to cover how to manage a project, but to discuss a way to incorporate responsiveness and performance into a project plan. With a responsive project plan we can communicate meaningful milestones to our stakeholders, without sacrificing all of the device experiences that we want to cover as part of our final product.

# [ 4 ]

# The Backend

THE THESIS OF THIS chapter—and really that of the entire book—is that to think about responsive web design as a frontend-only skill set is to limit the scope of what you can do and what tools are available to you. We are web developers, and as such we should be able to take advantage of the entire web stack in everything that we do. This chapter outlines how we can start thinking responsively from the backend.

## The Web Stack

Before we begin, I should define what the web stack is, because it is in fact a collection of several stacks. And, as we are talking about the Web, let's start with the network stack.

### THE NETWORK STACK

The network stack is a collection of protocols that outline how networked systems communicate. It is made up of the following layers:

*Data link layer*

This usually corresponds the standard way that hardware connects to the network. For our purposes, this is either via Ethernet, specifically the IEEE 802.3 standard for physically interconnected devices (*http://bit.ly/ethernet-standards*), or via WiFi, specifically the IEEE 802.11 standard for wirelessly interconnected devices (*http://bit. ly/1p8UW6P*).

*Network layer*

This layer corresponds to the standards that define communication and identification of nodes on a network, specifically the protocol IP, or Internet Protocol. It is through the Internet Protocol that nodes are identified via IP addresses and data is sent via packets between these hosts. The standard for Internet Protocol is maintained in IETF RFC 794, which you can read at *http://bit.ly/11j3ouQ*.

*Transport layer*

This usually corresponds to TCP, or Transmission Control Protocol, defined in IETF RFC 793 (*http://www.ietf.org/rfc/rfc793.txt*). TCP is the protocol used to establish connections between hosts. Whereas IP handles transmitting the data as packets, TCP divides the packets into segments, attaches headers to each segment to identify the destination IP address of the segment, and re-assembles and verifies the segments upon delivery.

*Application layer*

This top layer corresponds to HTTP, or Hyper Text Transport Protocol. The standard for HTTP is IETF RFC 2616, which you can see at *http://tools.ietf.org/html/rfc2616*. HTTP is the language of the Web, made up of verbs that make up the request/response structure.

Together this stack represents the steps that are traversed when sending and receiving data over the Internet, as illustrated in Figure 4-1.

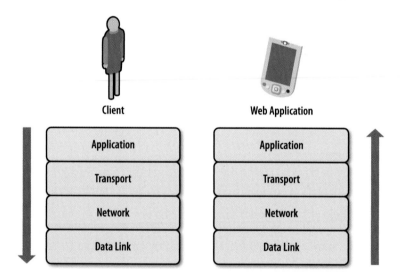

**FIGURE 4-1**

A user sending a request down the TCP/IP stack, and the same request traversing up the TCP/IP stack to make it to the web application residing on a remote server

## THE APPLICATION LAYER

Knowledge of all of the stacks is important, but for our purposes, as web developers, the primary layer with which we interface and have programmatic control is in the application layer, specifically HTTP.

Chapter 2 shows that an HTTP transaction happens within a TCP connection. It consists of a request from a client and a response from a server, but let's take a deeper dive into what constitutes a request and a response.

### The HTTP Request

An HTTP request is made up of two parts: a request line, and a set of request headers. The request line specifies the HTTP method, or verb, used in the request as well as the URI of the requested resource; or more plainly, it specifies what action I am looking to perform (get a file, send a file, get information about a file) and where I am looking to perform this action (the location of the file or resource). The following are some of the methods that are supported in HTTP 1.1:

*OPTIONS*
Queries the HTTP request methods that a server will support.

*GET*
Requests a remote resource. This becomes a conditional GET when you specify If-Modified-Since, If-Unmodified-Since, If-Match, If-None-Match, or If-Range in the HTTP header section, at which point the server will only return the resource if it has satisfied those requirements. Usually, you use conditional GETs when checking whether to retrieve a new asset or use the asset currently in cache.

*HEAD*
Requests only the HTTP header of a remote resource. This is used mainly to check the last modified date or to confirm that a URI is valid.

*POST*
Requests that the server update or modify an existing resource.

*PUT*
Requests that the server create a new resource.

*DELETE*
Requests that the server remove a resource.

The request header allows the client to specify parameters that augment the request, similar to how you can pass in parameters to a function. The following are some of the more interesting request headers:

*Host*
> The domain name specified in the URI.

*If-Modified-Since*
> This instructs the server to return the asset only if it has been updated since the date specified in this request header field. If the asset has been updated the server should respond with the asset and a status of 200; if it has not, the server simply responds with a status of 304.

*User-Agent*
> A string that identifies characteristics of the client making the request. This is the header that we will make the most use of this chapter.

By using network tracing tools such as Charles or Fiddler, you can inspect the contents of an HTTP request. The following example shows an HTTP request:

```
GET /style/base.css HTTP/1.1
Host: www.tom-barker.com
User-Agent: Mozilla/5.0 (Macintosh; Intel Mac OS X 10.7;
rv:27.0) Gecko/20100101 Firefox/27.0
Accept: text/css,*/*;q=0.1
Accept-Language: en-US,en;q=0.5
Accept-Encoding: gzip, deflate
Referer: http://www.tom-barker.com/blog/?p=x
Connection: keep-alive
```

### The HTTP Response

When the server receives and processes a request, it sends a response to the client that issued the request. Just like the HTTP request, the HTTP response is made up of two parts: the status line and the header fields.

The status line lists the protocol version (HTTP 1.1), the status code, and a textual phrase that describes the status of the request.

The status codes consist of three-digit numeric values that are broken up into five distinct high-level categories of response. The first digit of the status code indicates its category. Per the W3C's HTTP specification, which you can reference at *http://bit.ly/rfc-http*, the categories are the following:

*1xx: Informational*
> Request received, continuing process

*2xx: Success*
> The action was successfully received, understood, and accepted

*3xx: Redirection*
> Further action must be taken to complete the request

*4xx: Client Error*
> The request contains bad syntax or cannot be fulfilled

*5xx: Server Error*
> The server failed to fulfill an apparently valid request

The header fields are much like the request headers in that they are passed name-value pairs with which the server can specify additional information about the response. Here are some of the more interesting response headers are:

*Age*
> Denotes the server's estimate of the amount of time since the requested resource was created or update.

*ETag*
> Lists the entity tag identifier that the server assigns to a resource. This is useful for conditional matching.

*Vary*
> Indicates what request headers should be used to determine if a request can be served by cache. Later in the chapter, we look at sending different responses from the server based on user agent information. The Vary header is important because it allows us to specify the User-Agent request header to be part of the cache evaluation.

Here's a sample HTTP response:

```
HTTP/1.1 200 OK
Date: Sat, 29 Mar 2014 19:53:24 GMT
Server: Apache
Last-Modified: Sat, 05 May 2012 22:11:12 GMT
Content-Length: 2599
Keep-Alive: timeout=10, max=100
Connection: Keep-Alive
Content-Type: text/css
```

## CHARLES

There are a number of tools available for inspecting your network traffic. There are the in-browser developer tools (covered in Chapter 2), but there are also more in-depth traffic analysis tools; one of the favorites among web developers is Charles (see Figure 4-2).

Charles is an HTTP monitoring tool that you can use to watch and edit HTTP traffic over the network. Charles is also an HTTP proxy that you can use to throttle the bandwidth and latency of connections, intercept requests, spoof DNS calls, and even map local files to appear as if they are part of a remote website. Charles is available to download from *http://www.charlesproxy.com/*.

**FIGURE 4-2**

The Charles home page

Figure 4-3 depicts the Charles interface. This particular screenshot is showing all of the transactions that were recorded in a given section, in sequence; note the fields that are exposed, including HTTP status, HTTP method, host, payload of the transaction, and duration.

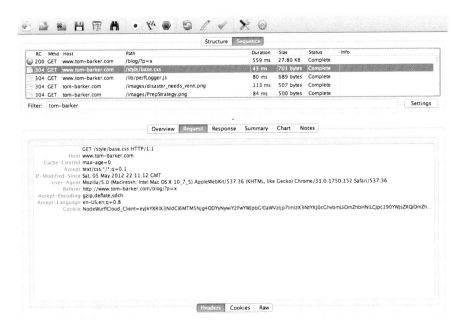

**FIGURE 4-3**
HTTP transactions recorded in Charles

# Web Application Stack

So far, we've talked about the underlying infrastructure and networking protocols on which our web applications run. Let's make sure we understand the software stack that our web applications run on.

Most, if not all, web applications operate in a client-server model, which is just a distributed computing methodology in which, if I were to describe it in grossly oversimplified terms, clients request data from servers. Servers process the requests and respond; oftentimes, these servers are distributed across a network for the sake of scalability.

In the interest of giving concrete examples of this model, let's assume that a browser is a client, and a web server is a server. When I say web server, I can be referring to either a piece of software such as Apache (*https://httpd.apache.org/*) or Microsoft's Internet Information Server (*http://www.iis.net/*), or I can be referring to the actual hardware on which the software runs on.

Continuing with our example scenario, the web servers listen on certain ports—application endpoints denoted by number—for HTTP requests to come in; HTTP requests come in on port 80, and HTTPS requests come in on port 443. When the web server gets a request it routes the request to the appropriate resource.

The resource could be code that is evaluated and interpreted on the server side, as in the case of Ruby or PHP, or it could be static content such as an HTML page. Either way, the routed request is met with a response from the server that goes back to the client.

In the case of a response that has an HTML document as its body, the HTML is parsed and rendered on the client device. If there is any JavaScript on the page, that is interpreted on the client side as well.

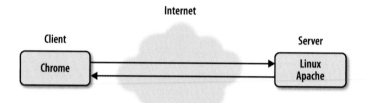

**FIGURE 4-4**

An example of a client-server transaction

## Responding on the Server Side

Now that you understand the protocol and software stacks in the web stack, the first thing you should establish is the earliest point in the stack at which you can determine client capabilities. Right now, the norm for responsive design is to determine client capabilities on the client side after the server has sent the HTTP response and the client has received, parsed, and rendered contents of the response. Architecturally, that looks like Figure 4-5, in which the browser requests the page; the web server receives the request at port 80 and passes it to the web application, the web application processes the request and responds, the client receives the response, parses the page, renders the page, runs the code on the client device to determine capabilities, and then finally reacts appropriately based on those capabilities.

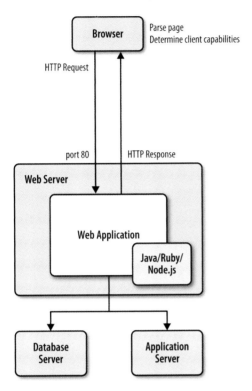

**FIGURE 4-5**
Determining capabilities on the client side

Even just describing all of that in written words feels overly and unnecessarily complicated.

But what we can glean from the HTTP request description is that the user agent is passed to the web server and the web application, and that the user agent describes the client. We could instead push the logic to determine client capabilities to our backend, our server side. This would make it possible for us to streamline what we send to the client, sending device-specific code instead of all of the code for all of the devices (see Figure 4-6 for what that amended architecture would look like).

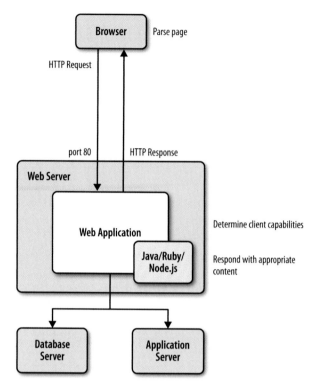

**FIGURE 4-6**

Determining client capabilities on the server-side and responding with device appropriate content

To understand how we determine client capabilities based on the User Agent, let's first take a look at the User Agent.

### INSPECTING THE USER AGENT

The specification for the User Agent field is defined in section 14.43 of RFC 2616, the HTTP specification, which you can read at *http://bit. ly/1tDGOZ0.*

The User Agent is a string that is composed of different tokens that describe the browser, browser version, and system information such as operating system and version. Some example User Agent strings are presented in Table 4-1.

**TABLE 4-1.** Sample User Agent strings by browser type

| BROWSER | USER AGENT STRING |
|---------|-------------------|
| Chrome 34 on a Mac | Mozilla/5.0 (Macintosh; Intel Mac OS X 10_7_5) AppleWebKit/537.36 (KHTML, like Gecko) Chrome/34.0.1847.116 Safari/537.36 |
| Safari on an iPhone running OS 7 | Mozilla/5.0 (iPhone; CPU iPhone OS 7_0 like Mac OS X) AppleWebKit/537.51.1 (KHTML, like Gecko) Version/7.0 Mobile/11A465 Safari/9537.53 |
| Safari on an iPad running OS 6 | Mozilla/5.0 (iPad; CPU OS 6_0 like Mac OS X) AppleWebKit/536.26 (KHTML, like Gecko) Version/6.0 Mobile/10A5355d Safari/8536.25 |
| Chrome on an Android phone running Ice Cream Sandwich | Mozilla/5.0 (Linux; U; Android 4.0.3; ko-kr; LG-L160L Build/IML74K) AppleWebkit/534.30 (KHTML, like Gecko) Version/4.0 Mobile Safari/534.30 |

You can fairly easily parse the string and pull out the relevant information by using regular expressions. As an example, you could craft a function to determine an idea of the client device, and from there establish an idea of client capabilities. A simple example, using JavaScript, of a function that checks for mobile devices might look like the following:

```
function detectMobileDevice(ua){
    var re = new RegExp(/iPhone|iPod|iPad|Android/);
    if(re.exec(ua)){
        return true;
    }else{
        return false;
    }
}
```

Note that we pass the User Agent into the detectMobileDevice() function, search through the User Agent with a regular expression for instances of the strings iPhone, iPad, or Android, and return true if any of those strings are found.

This is a fairly rudimentary example that only cares about the platform or operating system of the client device. A much more robust example would check for capabilities, such as touch support, and for the maximum size that a device would support.

Both Google and Apple publish their User Agent string standards at *http://bit.ly/1u0cHqv* and *http://bit.ly/ZXVAhT*, respectively

A word of caution about the reliability of User Agent strings: when reading the specification, you will notice that clients SHOULD include the User Agent information with their request. That is a very explicit declaration in the spec, in fact SHOULD is listed as a keyword by the IETF and there is a specification around what keywords mean, which you can see at *http://tools.ietf.org/html/rfc2119*. The specification for the word SHOULD states the following:

> ... there may exist valid reasons in particular circumstances to ignore a particular item, but the full implications must be understood and carefully weighed before choosing a different course.

Stated plainly, this just means that clients are not obligated to use the User Agent field, or even to correctly represent themselves with the correct User Agent. Users can spoof their User Agent if they choose to, bots or spiders can and often will give unexpected results. But these are the exceptions, and when developing for the general public there is nothing wrong with trusting what you get as the User Agent. The biggest pain point with User Agents is keeping current with all of the new ones as they come out, and being able to correlate User Agents to a known feature and capability set. Which is why we may want to use a device detection service.

## DEVICE DETECTION SERVICES

The previous example is great if we only care to establish that our clients are coming from a known set of devices, but what if we wanted to instead check for the capabilities and size of the devices? We could either use the User Agent to look up a table of our own design that lists User Agents and client capabilities, or we could take advantage of a service that provides that table and look-up capability for us.

There are several such services, called *device detection services*, to which we can pass the request to ascertain the client's capabilities for us.

The architecture for such a solution is depicted in Figure 4-7, where client requests come over the Internet, are received by our server, and at the server level we make a back door call out to the device detection service.

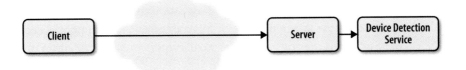

**FIGURE 4-7**
Using a device detection service from the server side

One of the oldest and widely used device detection services is theWurfl.

## The Wurfl

Prior to 2011, the Wurfl, which stands for Wireless Universal Resource FiLe, was an open and freely available XML file that listed devices and capabilities. It looked something like the following:

```
<device id="generic_android_ver3_0" user_agent="DO_NOT_MATCH_
ANDROID_3_0" fall_back="generic_android_ver2_4">
  <group id="product_info">
   <capability name="is_tablet" value="true"/>
   <capability name="device_os_version" value="3.0"/>
   <capability name="can_assign_phone_number" value="false"/>
   <capability name="release_date" value="2011_february"/>
  </group>
  <group id="streaming">
   <capability name="streaming_preferred_protocol" val-
ue="http"/>
  </group>
  <group id="display">
   <capability name="columns" value="100"/>
   <capability name="physical_screen_height" value="217"/>
   <capability name="dual_orientation" value="true"/>
   <capability name="physical_screen_width" value="136"/>
   <capability name="rows" value="100"/>
   <capability name="max_image_width" value="980"/>
   <capability name="resolution_width" value="1280"/>
   <capability name="resolution_height" value="768"/>
   <capability name="max_image_height" value="472"/>
  </group>
  <group id="sms">
   <capability name="sms_enabled" value="false"/>
  </group>
  <group id="xhtml_ui">
   <capability name="xhtml_send_mms_string" value="none"/>
   <capability name="xhtml_send_sms_string" value="none"/>
  </group>
</device>
```

Since 2011, however, the founders of the Wurfl formed the company Scientiamobile to provide services based around the Wurfl and ceased supporting the open document for individual consumption. They instead provide a series of products around the Wurfl, including Wurfl Cloud, which provides access to the device database via an API; Wurfl Onsite, which is a local install of the device database; and Wurfl Infuze, which makes the Wurf database available via environmental variables on the server side.

In theory, the best performing solution should be Wurfl Infuze because there would be no file I/O or transactional latency costs involved when querying for device data. But the solution with the lowest barrier to entry—because it involves no internal hosting, no infrastructure setup, and even has a free option—is the Wurfl Cloud. As such, we will look at how to integrate with the Wurfl Cloud in this chapter.

To begin, take a moment and go to the Scientiamobile home page at *http://www.scientiamobile.com/*, which you can see in Figure 4-8.

**FIGURE 4-8**

Scientiamobile home page

From there, we can click on the Wurfl Cloud link at the bottom of the page, which takes us to a pricing page. We can click on the Sign Up link under the free option, which takes us to the page we can see in Figure 4-9, where we create our account. This screen is available at *http://bit.ly/1x34Psg*.

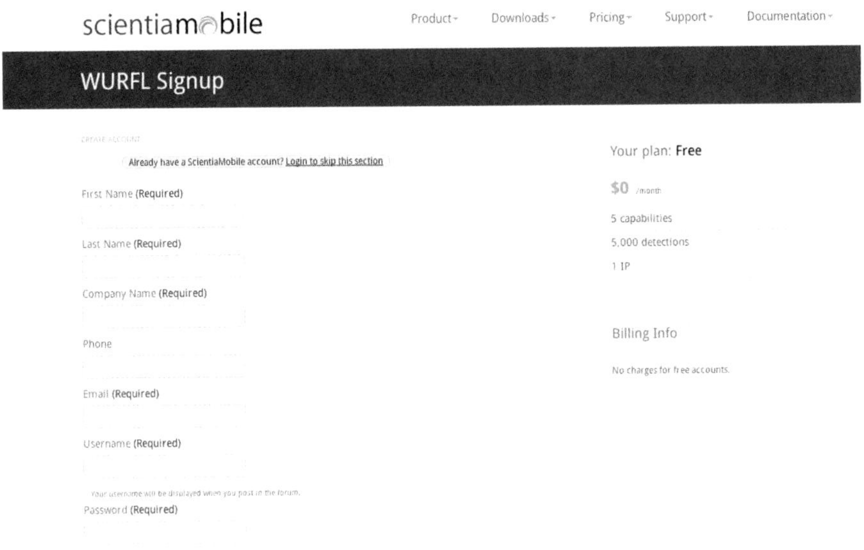

scientiamobile    Product▾    Downloads▾    Pricing▾    Support▾    Documentation▾

**WURFL Signup**

CREATE ACCOUNT
Already have a ScientiaMobile account? Login to skip this section

First Name (Required)

Last Name (Required)

Company Name (Required)

Phone

Email (Required)

Username (Required)

Your username will be displayed when you post in the forum.
Password (Required)

Your plan: **Free**

$0 /month

5 capabilities
5,000 detections
1 IP

Billing Info

No charges for free accounts.

**FIGURE 4-9**
Signing up for an account

After you have set up an account, you need to get an API key. You can do this on the Account Settings page, shown in Figure 4-10.

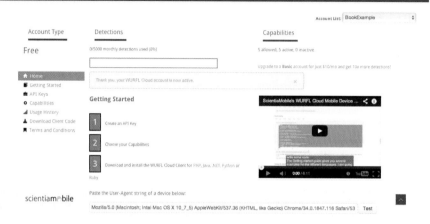

**FIGURE 4-10**

Configuring our account in the account settings page

From the Account Settings page, you can also choose what device capabilities you will want to be able to test for (the free account offers only five capabilities). To choose capabilities, drag them from an available capabilities list to your own selected capabilities list. The names of the capabilities will also be how you reference them in your code, as you can see in Figure 4-11.

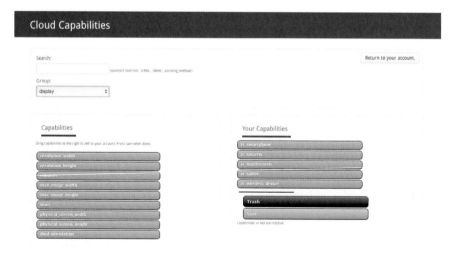

**FIGURE 4-11**

Selecting capabilities that you are checking for from the Wurfl Cloud

The final step you will need to take will be to download the Wurlf Cloud client code for the language that you will be using and then start to code your solution. As of this writing, the Wurfl Client code is available for the following languages and technologies:

- Java
- PHP
- Microsoft .Net
- Python
- Ruby
- Node.js
- Perl

Figure 4-12 depicts the Wurfl Cloud client download page.

**FIGURE 4-12**
Choosing the Wurfl Cloud client that is right for you

The Wurfl Cloud client downloads as a ZIP file and contains classes that you can use in your projects to interface with the Wurfl Cloud.

## Sample Code

Let's next take a look at how we can create an application that uses the Wurfl Cloud. Before we dive into the code, let's first cover some assumptions.

You will use Node.js and have downloaded the Wurfl Cloud client for Node.js. The Wurfl Cloud client comes in a ZIP file that you just have unzipped and placed somewhere that is accessible to the Node.js application. Like most Node.js applications, you already have a server.js that listens for incoming requests and a *router.js* that routes requests appropriately. You already have an *index.js* file that pulls together your *server.js* and application logic (from a file named *responsiveApp.js* that you will be creating shortly). Here's the content of *index.js*:

```
var server = require('./server/server.js');
var router = require('./server/router.js');
var responsiveApp = require("./responsiveApp.js");

var handle = {}
handle["/"] = responsiveApp.start;
handle["/start"] = responsiveApp.start;
handle["/favicon.ico"] = responsiveApp.favicon;

server.start(router.route, handle);
```

The *index.js* file loads the *server.js* and *router.js* files, as well as the *responsiveApp.js* file (even though you haven't yet created it). It creates an object that you call handle and then pass into the server to instruct it how to handle paths that could be called; in this example, we just map all requests (except the favicon request) to the start function in the *responsiveApp.js* file. And finally, you call the **server.start** function to get started.

The **server.start** function just creates an event handler that fires whenever HTTP requests come in. The event handler passes requests to *router.js*, which examines the request, compares it to the handler object, and calls the appropriate function.

Exploring a deep dive into Node.js is beyond the scope of this book, if you would like further reading to learn more about Node.js definitely check out *Learning Node* by Shelley Powers (O'Reilly).

OK, let's create the application logic that will reside in the *responsiveApp.js* file. First, load the HTTP module. Then load the two main files that came with the download (i.e., *WurflCloudClient.js* and *Config.js*):

```
var http = require('http');
var wurfl_cloud_client = require("./NodeWurflCloudClient/Wurfl
CloudClient");
var config = require("./NodeWurflCloudClient/Config");
```

Next, we'll create the start function, but we will have it just call a function that we will create called getCapabilities. We will also create our favicon function to respond with our favicon file if we have one:

```
function start(response, request) {
  getCapabilities(response, request);
}

function favicon(response) {
  response.writeHead(200, {
'Content-Type': 'image/x-icon'
} );
//write favicon here
  response.end();
}
```

Now let's get to the meat of the functionality. We'll create our get-Capabilities function. Remember that the start function passes the response and request objects into this function:

```
function getCapabilities(response, request) {

}
```

We'll begin by creating two variables: one an object that called result_capabilities, and the other an array that we'll call request_capabilities. The request_capabilities array lists out the capabilities for which we want to check—the same capabilities that you configured in your Wurfl account earlier in the chapter:

```
function getCapabilities(response, request) {
  var result_capabilities = {};
  var request_capabilities = ['is_smartphone','is_tablet',
'is_touchscreen', 'is_wireless_device']
```

Create a variable called api_key in which you enter the API key that you got from the Wurfl Account Configuration screen. We will also create a variable called configuration that will hold the configuration object that is returned when we call config.WurflCloudConfig with the API key:

```
  var api_key = "XXXXX ";
  var configuration = new config.WurflCloudConfig(api_key);
```

We will next instantiate an instance of wurfl_cloud_client.WurflCloudClient with the configuration object (with the API key) and the request and the response objects all passed in. Call this object WurflCloudClientObject.

This object is the key to accessing the capabilities from the Wurfl. We need to call the detectDevice method of that objet, pass in the request, request_capabilities, and an anonymous function that will be fired when the results of our query return:

```
WurflCloudClientObject.detectDevice(request, request_capabili-
ties, function(err, result_capabilities){
```

Within that anonymous function, we will put our logic to render the correct HTML, CSS, and JavaScript tailored for that experience. In our simplified example, we are just calling functions that will output the correct data (drawSmartphoneHomepage, etc.), but with the idea being that instead of putting all of our device- or experience-specific code in media queries and as part of client-side interpretation, we instead have the server output only the device- or experience-specific code in this branching logic:

```
if(err!=null){
    console.log("<br>Error: " + err + " <br/>");
}
else{
    if(result_capabilities['is_smartphone']){
        drawSmartphoneHomepage(response);
    }else if(result_capabilities['is_tablet']){
        drawTabletHomepage(response);
    }else{
        drawDesktopHomepage(response);
    }

}
```

For reference, the complete code example looks like the following:

```
var http = require('http');
var wurfl_cloud_client = require("./NodeWurflCloudClient/Wurfl
CloudClient");
var config = require("./NodeWurflCloudClient/Config");

function start(response, request) {
  getCapabilities(response, request);
}

function favicon(response) {
  response.writeHead(200, {
'Content-Type': 'image/x-icon'
} );
//write favicon here
  response.end();
}
```

```
function getCapabilities(response, request) {
  var result_capabilities = {};
  var request_capabilities = ['is_smartphone','is_tablet',
'is_touchscreen', 'is_wireless_device']
  var api_key = "XXXXX ";
  var configuration = new config.WurflCloudConfig(api_key);
  var WurflCloudClientObject = new wurfl_cloud_client.Wurfl-
CloudClient(configuration, request, response);
  WurflCloudClientObject.detectDevice(request, request_capa-
bilities, function(err, result_capabilities){
        console.log(result_capabilities);
    if(err!=null){
      console.log("<br>Error: " + err + " <br/>");
    }
    else{
        if(result_capabilities['is_smartphone']){
            drawSmartphoneHomepage(response);
        }else if(result_capabilities['is_tablet']){
            drawTabletHomepage(response);
        }else{
            drawDesktopHomepage(response);
        }
        }

  });
}

exports.start = start;
exports.favicon = favicon;
exports.getCapabilities = getCapabilities;
```

## Implications of Cache

When you develop websites for an enormous scale, you tend to rely very heavily on cache to minimize the hits to your origin servers. The danger here is that when we move our responsiveness to the server side but we are caching our responses, we serve the cached version of whatever our last response was, regardless of what the User Agent information being passed in from the client is.

To get around this, we can use the Vary HTTP response header when sending our responses from the server. This informs the cache layers that the server does some negotiating based on the User Agent string, and to cache responses based on the User Agent field when requests come in.

## Edge Side Includes

Using CDNs such as Akamai to serve your content cached from the edge is a great strategy to reduce traffic to your origin servers. This lessens the amount of hardware that you need to maintain, and makes it possible for you to deliver content to your end users much faster.

Figure 4-13 provides a high-level overview of what this architecture might look like.

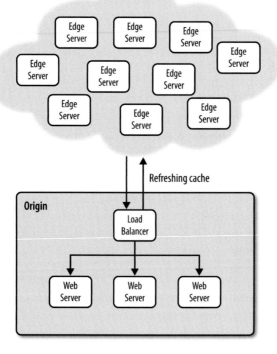

**FIGURE 4-13**

Serving cached content from an edge network

As just stated a moment ago, the problem we could run into with this architecture is that if the CDN provider doesn't allow us to cache User Agent–specific content (again by using the Vary HTTP header), all of our clients will get the same cached content, not device-specific content.

A solution around this is to use Edge Side Include (ESI) language. ESI was created by a consortium of companies, including Akamai and Oracle, and submitted to the W3C. You can read the specification for ESI at *http://bit.ly/1rY5WUO*.

ESI is a mark-up–based language that is embedded inline in an HTML document. The edge servers have an ESI processor that reads the ESI tags, interprets the logic, and renders the output inline in the HTML. ESI functions very much like a server-side scripting language such as PHP that can be interpreted on the server side and output inline in the HTML. Just like PHP, the ESI tags are not shown to the client; only their output is rendered.

The following code is an example of an ESI script that looks at incoming User Agent data and loads appropriate content:

```
<html>
<head></head>
<body>
<esi:choose>
 <esi:when test="$(HTTP_USER_AGENT{'os'})=='iPhone'">
     <esi:comment text="Include iPhone specific resources
here" />
     …
 </esi:when>
 <esi:when test="$(HTTP_USER_AGENT{'os'})=='iPad'">
     <esi:comment text="Include iPad specific resources here"
/>
     …
 </esi:when>
 <esi:when test="$(HTTP_USER_AGENT{'os'})=='Android'">
     <esi:comment text="Include Android specific resources
here" />
     …
 </esi:when>
 <esi:otherwise>
     <esi:comment text="Include desktop specific resources
here" />
     …
 </esi:otherwise>
</esi:choose>
</body>
</html>
```

## Summary

This chapter widened the lens through which we look at our applications. We explored the protocol and software stack on which our applications reside, and over which transactions to and from our applications need to traverse. With this larger perspective, we asked this question: how soon from the user's initial request can we know the capabilities of the client device, and most important, how soon can we begin to act upon that request?

To answer that question we looked at inspecting the User Agent field of the incoming HTTP request, and even utilizing a third-party device detection service such as the Wurlf.

One potential pitfall of this solution is how to handle highly cached content. One solution is to use the Vary HTTP response header to instruct our cache servers that responses should be cached differently based on the User Agent. Another solution is to push the device or capabilities detection logic from our origin servers out to our CDN edge servers by using ESI.

Whatever our solution, if we can push our responsiveness upstream in the HTTP transaction, to the server (or edge) and not have it all take place on the client side, we can avoid the anti-patterns of serving double the content or extraneous content in our payload to the client, instead serving a more streamlined tailored response that perform better because it is respectful of both the bandwidth, battery life, and CPU limitations of the end user's device.

# [ 5 ]

# The Frontend

CHAPTER 4 EXPLORES HOW TO MIGRATE THE RESPONSIVENESS PARA-
DIGM FROM THE CLIENT SIDE TO THE BACKEND. The concept is two-fold:
first, load device-appropriate content and serve a dedicated experience
from the backend; second, avoid the anti-pattern of loading the content
for all devices. This lowers the overall payload of the page, and reduces
what the client device has to do to finally render a page.

But what if your infrastructure, business model, or team's skill set
aren't conducive to a server-side solution? In this case, there are ways
to achieve similar performance gains from purely client-side solutions.

In this chapter, we direct our focus back to the frontend and discuss
other ways to facilitate the same patterns.

## Working with Images

As Steve Souders shows us via his Interesting Stats page in the HTTP
Archive, the biggest contributor to page payload are the images on a
page (see Figure 5-1). Thus, arguably the biggest impact we can have on
responsive performance from the client side is to optimize the delivery
of images to mobile clients.

Responsive images in the past have been looked at as needing to scale
with a page as the viewport shrinks. Chapter 1 presents a competitive
analysis that illustrates how this has usually been achieved by either
just resizing images via CSS, or saving images twice as large as necessary and then scaling them down via CSS. But again, these solutions
are actually performance anti-patterns: loading the same assets for all
devices, and loading assets at twice the size.

For a site to be truly responsive to users' performance needs—including bandwidth constraints, battery life, pixel density, and viewport
size—we must instead follow the pattern of loading device appropriate
assets.

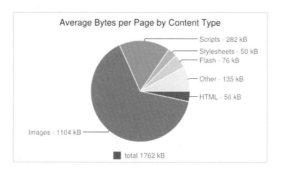

**FIGURE 5-1**

From the HTTP Archive, accounting for how page payload is distributed across resource types

This aspect of responsiveness, specifically responsive images, is clearly an area in need of standardization, as evidenced by the proposed solutions currently in working-draft status. Let's take a look at these, as well as some other options.

## THE SRCSET ATTRIBUTE

One of the current options in draft to serve responsive images is the srcset attribute for the <img> tag, recently added by the W3C. The draft for the srcset attribute is available at *http://bit.ly/1tDH5Lr*. At a high level, the srcset attribute is an update to the <img> tag by which you can specify different images to use for the different pixel ratios of client devices. Let's take a look at what exactly that means.

```
<img src="1x.jpg" srcset="2x.jpg 2x">
```

### Device Pixel Ratio

Looking at the preceding source code, you can see that a default image, *1x.jpg*, is specified in the src attribute of the <img> tag. The default is there for backward compatibility, in case the browser doesn't support srcset. Then, you set the srcset attribute and point to a different image—in this case, *2x.jpg*—that the browser should use if the device pixel ratio is 2.

Device pixel ratio is the ratio between physical pixels and device-independent pixels on a device. The classic example is of an iPad Retina display being 1,024 physical pixels wide, but because it is a Retina display, it packs more informational pixels, or device-independent pixels, so it has an actual pixel width of 2,048. So, the calculation to determine the device pixel ratio for a Retina display iPad would be the following:

[device independent pixels] divided by [physical pixels]

or

2,048/1,024 = 2

If you'd like to read more about this, try Peter-Paul Koch's in-depth Quirksmode.org article at *http://bit.ly/1uBP6R1*.

The value of a device's pixel ratio is exposed to the browser via the window.devicePixelRatio property. Figure 5-2 offers a screenshot of our srcset example, in which we see Google Chrome emulating a Motorola Droid Razr HD, which has a devicePixelRatio of 1.

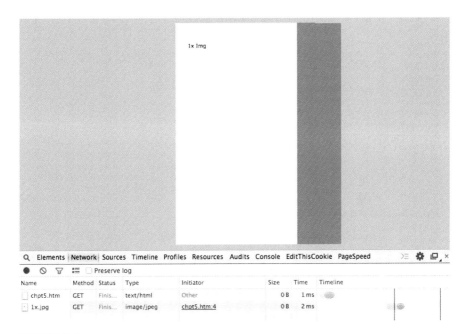

**FIGURE 5-2**
Emulating a Motorola Droid Razr HD

The Droid Razr HD has a 720 × 1280 resolution display and a devicePixelRatio of 1, causing our 1x image to be loaded. Here is the User Agent string:

```
Mozilla/5.0 (Linux; U; Android 2.3; en-us; DROID RAZR 4G
Build/6.5.1-73_DHD-11_M1-29) AppleWebKit/533.1 (KHTML, like
Gecko) Version/4.0 Mobile Safari/533.1
```

Figure 5-3 shows Chrome emulating an iPad 4 which has a Retina display and a `devicePixelRatio` of 2.

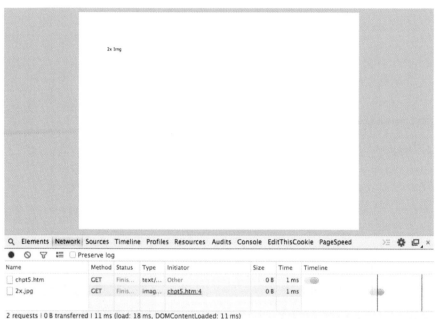

**FIGURE 5-3**
Emulating an Apple iPad 4

The Apple iPad 4 has a resolution of 2,048 × 1,536 and a `devicePixel Ratio` of 2, causing our 2x image to be loaded. Following is the User Agent string for the iPad:

```
Mozilla/5.0 (iPad; CPU OS 7_0 like Mac OS X) AppleWebKit/
537.51.1 (KHTML, like Gecko) Version/7.0 Mobile/11A465 Safari/
9537.53.
```

In both of the previous examples, we can see on the Network tab in Developer Tools that only the required image file is downloaded. Also note in both screenshots that these are emulated devices. Full support for the `srcset` attribute is still being rolled out, and you are advised to check your usage logs to get a list of your top devices and test on those devices to ensure that they support the `srcset` attribute.

The downside of using the srcset attribute is that you are sending extraneous bytes in the payload by specifying all of the different images we might need. If you're interested in optimizing even further, Ilya Grigorik, author of *High Performance Browser Networking* (O'Reilly), outlines an elegant way to move the mapping of the device pixel ratio to the backend, which you can see at *http://bit.ly/1qnPSeY*.

The upside of the srcset attribute, aside from making it possible for you to specify multiple images to use for device-specific requirements and not needing to download multiple images, is that it is starting to be supported in modern browsers unlike our next topic of discussion, the picture element.

## THE PICTURE ELEMENT

Another part of the proposed option for handling responsive images is the <picture> element. You can view the working draft from the W3C at *http://www.w3.org/TR/html-picture-element/*.

The <picture> element is a new element to be added to HTML5. Conceptually, it is a container element that holds different source tags that specify images to use based on device constraints, viewport width, and pixel density. It can also hold an <img> tag that allows for graceful fallback.

The <source> element supports a media attribute that specifies the media type and CSS property that you can target, and a src element that you can specify an image to download for that targeted media type and CSS property.

If you were to re-create the earlier srcset example in which we targeted high pixel density tablets and phones, using the <picture> element, it would look similar to the following:

```
<picture>
    <source media="(min-width: 640px, min-device-pixel-ratio:
2)" src=" hi-res_small.jpg ">
    <source media="(min-width: 2048px, min-device-pixel-ratio:
2)" src=" hi-res_large.jpg ">
    <img src="1x.png ">
</picture>
```

What makes the <picture> element really interesting is that is also supports the srcset attribute. The combination of the two would look like
the following:

```
<picture>
    <source srcset="big.jpg 1x, big-2x.jpg 2x, big-3x.jpg 3x"
type="image/jpeg" media="(min-width: 40em)" />
    <source srcset="med.jpg 1x, med-2x.jpg 2x, med-3x.jpg 3x"
type="image/jpeg" />
    <img src="fallback.jpg" alt="fancy pants" />
</picture>
```

Both the srcset attribute and the <picture> element are interesting
potential solutions. If we were to compare the two solutions from a
performance perspective, in theory they both should only download
the appropriate resource based on the client capabilities, but the <pic-
ture> element is clearly more verbose than simply using the <img> tag
with the srcset attribute. If we were to quantify that statement, just in
the examples that we've used so far in this chapter, the image with the
srcset attribute used 95 bytes, whereas the <picture> element example
used 231 bytes—the srcset example used 60 percent less bytes than
the <picture> element. Figure 5-4 presents a side-by-side comparison.

When viewed by themselves, the numbers 95 and 231 bytes seem fairly
innocuous. But that's for a single <img> tag. Take a moment to review
the data set for the Alexa top site in Chapter 1. If we were to use that
data set of websites, and pull just the <img> tags from all of those sites,
the data on the byte size would look like that shown in Table 5-1 (note
that those numbers are in kilobytes).

**TABLE 5-1.** Summary of byte size data set

| | |
|---|---|
| MIN. | 0.000 |
| 1ST QUARTILE | 0.305 |
| MEDIAN | 3.650 |
| MEAN | 56.507 |
| 3RD QUARTILE | 62.125 |
| MAX | 371.100 |

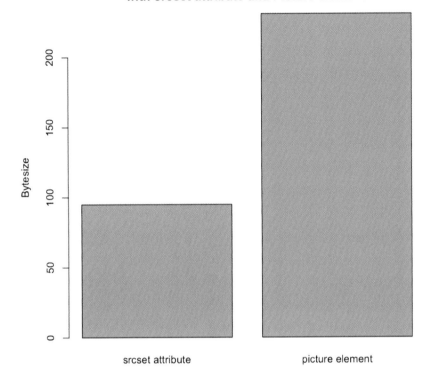

**Difference in bytesize using IMG element with srcset attribute and Picture element**

Bytesize

srcset attribute          picture element

**FIGURE 5-4**

Difference in byte size from the examples of using the IMG tag with the srcset attribute versus using the <picture> element to achieve the same ends

At the maximum, that is 371 kb just in <img> tag text, not counting any other HTML, CSS, or JavaScript on the page. Granted, some of that file size is most likely tracking beacons and spacers that wouldn't require multiple versions for different devices, but if we extrapolate those numbers, we get the performance implications shown in Figure 5-5 just for using the <picture> element instead of the <img> element.

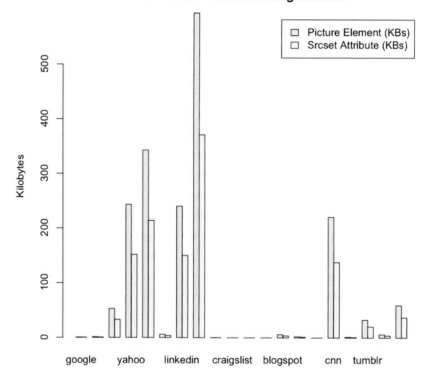

**Extrapolation of byte size comparison for Picture element vs Img element**

FIGURE 5-5

Extrapolation of byte size difference

With this extrapolation, the summary of our data using the <picture> element now looks like Table 5-2.

**TABLE 5-2.** Summary of extrapolated byte size data set

| MIN. | 0.000 |
|---|---|
| 1ST QUARTILE | 0.488 (+0.183 KB) |
| MEDIAN | 5.840 (+2.19 KB) |
| MEAN | 90.411 (+33.904 KB) |
| 3RD QUARTILE | 99.400 (+37.275 KB) |
| MAX | 593.760 (+222.66 KB) |

So, pragmatically, the increase in size for 75 percent of sites tested was smaller than if we were to load an additional image, but it's in the outliers that the concern could lie. Just look at our maximum size from the data set—it is now almost 600 KB! Clearly, although the <picture> element—at one time fully supported by modern browsers—will offer a robust way to load responsive images, because of its impact on file size of the page delivered, it should be treated as a potential solution for evaluation, not the default go-to solution for every responsive image.

It is important to note though that the trade-off of using the <picture> element in these examples would be additional tens of bytes of markup, whereas not using the picture element would be additional hundreds and thousands of bytes of images. Also, you can use compression to negate much of this impact to the payload.

## Lazy Loading

Thus far, we've touched upon images in this chapter. Let's now step back and look at how we might take a client-side approach to employing a strategy of only loading device-appropriate assets for the page that is being rendered. Chapter 1 demonstrates that from the perspective of the client-side, this solution would involve *lazy loading*.

With lazy loading, you load content only when it is actually needed. A familiar example of lazy loading is *infinite scroll*: only the content that is needed to draw "above the fold" (the content that is actually in view on a device) is brought in on page load, and more content is downloaded and rendered to the screen as a user scrolls. For our purposes, we might load in a bare-bones HTML skeletal structure with semantically structured content, determine the client capabilities, and then lazy load the associated CSS and JavaScript.

The architecture would look like Figure 5-6.

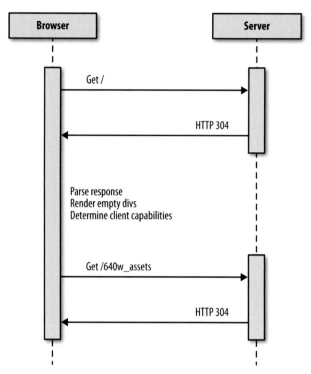

**FIGURE 5-6**

Lazy loading device appropriate content from the client-side

Let's take a look at an example. To begin, we'll start with our base HTML skeletal structure. We'll include only the bare minimum, no formatting, and only <div>s that have ids that indicate what content we will be loading into them (head, body, and footer, respectively):

```
<html>
<head></head>
<body>
<h2>Lazy Loading Example</h2>
<div id="head">
</div>
<div id="body">
    Loading Content
</div>
<div id="footer">
</div>
</body>
</html>
```

We will next make a <script> tag at the bottom of the body and create a function named determineClient(). Within determineClient, we will create an object named client that has its own object named sectionURLs, with the properties head, body, and footer, all named after the <div>s that we have on the page:

```
<script>
function determineClient(){
    var client = {
        sectionURLs: {
            head: "/components/head/",
            body: "/components/body/",
            footer: "/components/footer/"
        }
    };
}
</script>
```

The idea is that we will populate these properties with the URLs to the device- or experience-specific content after we have determined what those should be. We will create the object with default data in case we aren't able to determine capabilities.

Now, we'll add in some branching logic to test window.innerWidth and window.devicePixelRatio and populate the sectionURLs accordingly. For our example, we are assuming that we have directory structures set up based on sizes, such as those shown in Figure 5-7.

In Figure 5-7, there are directories with content for each viewport width, including directories for pixel-dense devices. Also note that each high-level section directory (head, body, footer) has its own *index.htm* files so that default content can be loaded. Of course, these don't need to be physical files as they are in the diagram; they can be Apache mod_rewrite rules or any other sort of URL manipulation that you want to implement.

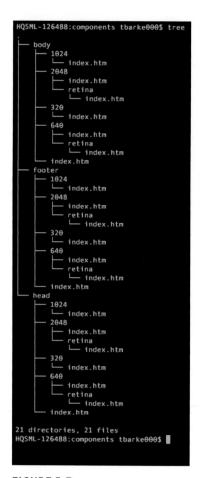

```
HQSML-126488:components tbarke000$ tree
.
├── body
│   ├── 1024
│   │   └── index.htm
│   ├── 2048
│   │   ├── index.htm
│   │   └── retina
│   │       └── index.htm
│   ├── 320
│   │   └── index.htm
│   ├── 640
│   │   ├── index.htm
│   │   └── retina
│   │       └── index.htm
│   └── index.htm
├── footer
│   ├── 1024
│   │   └── index.htm
│   ├── 2048
│   │   ├── index.htm
│   │   └── retina
│   │       └── index.htm
│   ├── 320
│   │   └── index.htm
│   ├── 640
│   │   ├── index.htm
│   │   └── retina
│   │       └── index.htm
│   └── index.htm
└── head
    ├── 1024
    │   └── index.htm
    ├── 2048
    │   ├── index.htm
    │   └── retina
    │       └── index.htm
    ├── 320
    │   └── index.htm
    ├── 640
    │   ├── index.htm
    │   └── retina
    │       └── index.htm
    └── index.htm

21 directories, 21 files
HQSML-126488:components tbarke000$ 
```

**FIGURE 5-7**

Directory structure of the example website

After our branching logic populates the client object, the `determine-Client()` function returns the client, as demonstrated here:

```
<script>
function determineClient(){
    var client = {
        sectionURLs: {
            head: "/components/head/",
            body: "/components/body/",
            footer: "/components/footer/"
        }
    };
```

```
        if(window.innerWidth == 320){
            client.sectionURLs.head = "/components/head/320/";
            client.sectionURLs.body = "/components/body/320/";
            client.sectionURLs.footer = "/components/footer/320/";
        }else if(window.innerWidth == 640){
            if(window.devicePixelRatio == 1){
                client.sectionURLs.head = "/components/head/640/";
                client.sectionURLs.body = "/components/body/640/";
                client.sectionURLs.footer = "/components/foot-
er/640/";
            }else if(window.devicePixelRatio >=2){
                client.sectionURLs.head = "/components/head/640/
retina/";
                client.sectionURLs.body = "/components/body/640/
retina/";
                client.sectionURLs.footer = "/components/footer/
640/retina/";
            }
        }else if((window.innerWidth == 1024) || (window.innerWidth
== 1440)){
            client.sectionURLs.head = "/components/head/1024/";
            client.sectionURLs.body = "/components/body/1024/";
            client.sectionURLs.footer = "/components/footer/
1024/";
        }else if(window.innerWidth == 2048){
            if(window.devicePixelRatio ==2){
                client.sectionURLs.head = "/components/head/2048/
retina/";
                client.sectionURLs.body = "/components/body/2048/
retina/";
                client.sectionURLs.footer = "/components/foot-
er/2048/retina/";
            }
        }
    return client;
}
</script>
```

If we were to output our client object to the console, it would look like the following:

```
Object {sectionURLs: Object}
sectionURLs: Object
body: "/components/body/1024/"
footer: "/components/footer/1024/"
head: "/components/head/1024/"
```

Next, we create a function named loadSection into which we pass the client object as well as a parameter that specifies the <div> that we will be targeting. This function is pretty much standard boilerplate XMLHttpRequest object code; to load in content from the server, our main customizations are the following:

- We create a section property on the xhr object ad hoc and assign it to the section parameter that has been passed into the function.

- In the callback function called when the data is loaded, we overwrite the innerHTML of the element with the ID that matches the section data with the responseText in our xhr object:

```
function loadSection(section, client){
var xhr = new XMLHttpRequest();
xhr.open("get", client.sectionURLs[section], true);
xhr.section = section;
xhr.send();
xhr.onload = function(){
    document.getElementById(xhr.section).innerHTML = xhr.
responseText;
    }
}
```

All that is left at this point is to wire all of this logic together. We will create a function that will execute when the window.load() event occurs, and this function will act as our controller, creating a variable to hold the client object passed out of our determineClient() function call, and then calling our loadSection() function for each section we have:

```
window.onload = function(){
    var client = determineClient();
    var sections = ["head", "body", "client"];
    for(var n=0;n<sections.length(),n++){
        loadSection(n, client);
    }
}
```

When we run this in a web browser, the Network tab should look similar to Figure 5-8.

Note that the base page loads and renders in 171 ms, whereas the lazy loaded content took an additional 131 ms to load.

**FIGURE 5-8**

Waterfall chart showing the head, body, and footer being lazy loaded after the page load

Following is the complete code example, which you can download from *http://tom-barker.com/demo/hprd/lazyload.htm*:

```
<html>
<head></head>
<body>
<h2>Lazy Loading Example</h2>
<div id="head">
</div>
<div id="body">
    Loading Content ...
</div>
<div id="footer">
</div>
<script>

window.onload = function(){
    var client = determineClient();
    var sections = ["head", "body", "client"];
    for(var n=0;n<sections.length(),n++){
        loadSection(n, client);
    }
}

    function loadSection(section, client){
        var xhr = new XMLHttpRequest();
        xhr.open("get", client.sectionURLs[section], true);
        xhr.section = section;
```

```
            xhr.send();
            xhr.onload = function(){
                document.getElementById(xhr.section).innerHTML =
xhr.responseText;
            }
        }

    function determineClient(){
    var client = {
        sectionURLs: {
            head: "/components/head/",
            body: "/components/body/",
            footer: "/components/footer/"
        }
    };
        if(window.innerWidth == 320){
            client.sectionURLs.head = "/components/head/320/";
            client.sectionURLs.body = "/components/body/320/";
            client.sectionURLs.footer = "/components/footer/
320/";
        }else if(window.innerWidth == 640){
            if(window.devicePixelRatio == 1){
                client.sectionURLs.head = "/components/
head/640/";
                client.sectionURLs.body = "/components/
body/640/";
                client.sectionURLs.footer = "/components/foot-
er/640/";
            }else if(window.devicePixelRatio >=2){
                client.sectionURLs.head = "/components/
head/640/retina/";
                client.sectionURLs.body = "/components/
body/640/retina/";
                client.sectionURLs.footer = "/components/foot-
er/640/retina/";
            }
        }else if((window.innerWidth == 1024) || (window.inner-
Width == 1440)){
            client.sectionURLs.head = "/components/
head/1024/";
            client.sectionURLs.body = "/components/
body/1024/";
            client.sectionURLs.footer = "/components/foot-
er/1024/";
        }else if(window.innerWidth == 2048){
            if(window.devicePixelRatio ==2){
                client.sectionURLs.head = "/components/
head/2048/retina/";
                client.sectionURLs.body = "/components/
body/2048/retina/";
```

```
                    client.sectionURLs.footer = "/components/foot-
er/2048/retina/";
                }
          }
          return client;
    }

</script>
</body>
</html>
```

Something else to keep in mind: the browser will automatically lazy
load CSS background images; if the display is set to none, the background image will not be loaded until the element is made visible. This
can be another tactic to lazy load certain images on the page.

## DEVICE DETECTION LIBRARIES

Testing capabilities is natural and easy on the client side, but it's still
difficult determining form factor and the exact device. You could make
the argument that as long as we know the capabilities, we don't need
to know the form factor, but that doesn't take into consideration things
such as network reliability. We could parse the User Agent to determine the form factor, but then we'd have to keep a look-up table to correlate tokens from the User Agent to specific devices and form factors.

What if instead of maintaining that look-up table, we wanted to rely on
a third party to do that? Relying on a third party would make it possible for us to accurately target specific form factors such as TVs without
having to maintain our own User Agent to device database. We could

again look to the world of device-detection databases. Both Wurfl and Device Atlas have client-side libraries that expose device capabilities within native JavaScript libraries. Device Atlas bundles its JavaScript library with its client download. Scientiamobile has a site, *http://wurfl. io/*, dedicated to distributing their client-side solution: *wurfl.js*. Figure 5-9 depicts the home page of *wurfl.io*.

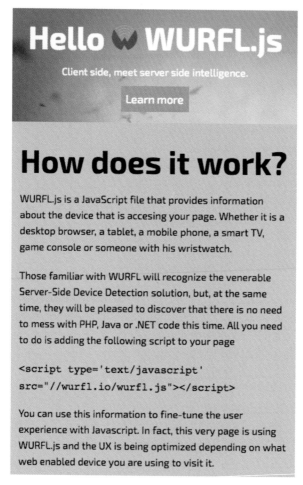

**FIGURE 5-9**
Scientiamobile's wurfl.io web page

To use the *wurfl.js*, simply include a link to the hosted JavaScript file:

```
<script type='text/javascript' src="http://wurfl.io/wurfl.js">
</script>
```

This creates an object in the global scope named WURFL. If you output the WURFL object to the console, it looks similar to the following:

```
>WURFL
Object {is_mobile: true, complete_device_name: "Apple iPad",
form_factor: "Tablet"}
```

As you can see, the WURFL object identifies whether a client is on a mobile device, the name of the device, and the device's form factor. Clearly this isn't a full capabilities list as much as it is an augmentation of the information we already have on the frontend.

The downside, of course, is that it involves an additional external call that our page needs to make, thus increasing the potential page payload and latency in delivering the page to our end users.

## Summary

This chapter focused your attention on the frontend of the web software stack. We first talked about the issue of responsive images and looked at new working drafts to the HTML5 standard to address responsive images. We compared the new srcset attribute in the <img> tag with the upcoming <picture> element and looked at the page payload implications of using them.

We then pulled back and looked at lazy loading entire sections of a page to avoid downloading unneeded styling and content. This was very much like the examples in Chapter 4 in which we employ the strategy of only loading device-appropriate content and formatting. But whereas Chapter 4 achieved this from the backend, the example in this chapter did so from the frontend.

There are advantages and disadvantages to either approach. When parsing the experience from the backend you need to be very aware and careful of your cache semantics because different experiences will be coming from the same URI. When parsing the experience from the frontend, you are at the mercy of the client device being able to run your code, and maintaining the network connection to load your additional assets.

In Chapter 6, we delve into continuous integration and talk about how to include checking responsiveness and the performance of our responsive sites into our continuous integration environment.

# [ 6 ]

# Continuous Web Performance Testing

## Maintaining a Steady Course

AS ANY STUDENT OF SYSTEMS THEORY KNOWS, when you've made a positive change to a system, you can maintain that change via feedback loops to check state and course correct as necessary. This is as true for a thermostat regulating the temperature of an area as it is to keep the web performance metrics of a website within range of an SLA during new feature development.

Essentially, feedback loops are tools used in control systems to assess the output of the system and thus correct the system's course if needed. At a very high level, they work like the flow shown in Figure 6-1, in which the output of a process is evaluated, giving feedback which becomes input that then feeds the process again.

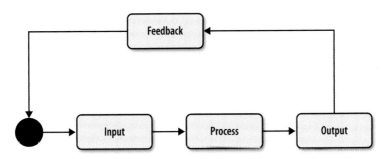

**FIGURE 6-1**
Basic feedback loop diagram

For software engineering, one of the most effective procedural feedback loops is the practice of *continuous integration*. Continuous integration (CI) is essentially having mechanisms in place that build your code as new code is committed, check for different success criteria, and break the build—effectively putting a stop to check-ins and deployments—until the success criteria is again satisfied. Figure 6-2 depicts the feedback look diagram updated to represent a continuous integration workflow.

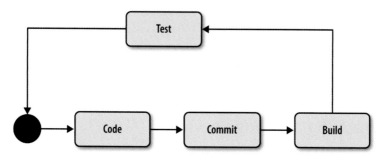

**FIGURE 6-2**
A CI feedback loop

At this point, you most likely have a CI environment set up in your department that is running automated tests against your builds. Maybe you use Jenkins or Anthill Pro or any other number of CI tools available. But I would bet that right now your automated test suite does not check for web performance or for web performance at different viewport sizes and different experiences. Let's change that.

## Automating Responsive Web Performance Testing

If we were talking web development 5 to 10 years ago, the concept of web–test-driven development was barely known. But over the last five-plus, years the idea of what is possible and what is mainstream around web–test-driven development has exploded.

Unit testing frameworks such as Jasmine from Pivotal Labs came out, and web developers began unit testing the logic in their JavaScript. Then, *headless web browser*[1] testing frameworks came out and demonstrated what could be done with integration testing.

---

1  A headless web browser is a web browser without a graphical user interface. With a headless web browser we can programmatically access web pages for tasks like testing and automation.

For the purposes of responsive web performance testing, headless web browsers are perfect because they do the following:

- Allow scripting of a browser from a terminal
- Integrate into CI software
- Allow automated resizing of the viewport
- Allow programmatic User Agent assignment
- Give insight into what assets are being loaded on a page

One of the most popular headless browser–testing libraries available is PhantomJS (*http://phantomjs.org*). PhantomJS is a JavaScript API created by Ariya Hidayat that exposes programmatic access to WebKit (or to be very specific, QtWebKit). Best of all, you can run PhantomJS from a command line, so you can integrate your tests into your CI workflow.

Let's take a look at how you can use PhantomJS to test website performance at different viewport sizes and with different User Agents.

## AUTOMATED HEADLESS BROWSER TESTING

First, you need to install PhantomJS. To do this, simply go to the console or terminal and type the following command:

```
sudo npm inst
all -g phantomjs
```

This installs PhantomJS at the global level so that we can run it no matter what directory we happen to be in. To ensure that PhantomJS is installed, check the version number from the command line, like so:

```
phantomjs --version
1.9.7
```

The core workflow when using PhantomJS is to create a page object and use that page object to load and analyze a web page:

```
var page = require('webpage').create();
page.open('http://localhost:8080/', function (status) {
});
```

The way to run this with PhantomJS is to save your code to a file and run the file from the command line:

```
>phantomjs filename.js
```

Functionality in PhantomJS is broken out into API modules that provide distinct areas of focus. The modules built into PhantomJS include the following:

*The System module*

This module makes it possible to, among other things, pull arguments from the command line so that you can make your scripts more generalized and simply pass in parameters such as lists of URLs (or viewport sizes, or paths to User Agent lists) instead of hard coding them in the script. We can also use the system module to access environmental variables and operating system information. To access the System module type the following:

```
var system = require('system');
console.log(system.args, system.env);
```

*The Web Page module*

Using this module, you can download and evaluate web pages. The beauty of the Web Page module is that in addition to giving you the ability to inspect a page and the network transactions that it took to create the page, you can also inject content into the page as well as insert HTTP header information when requesting the page. Here's how to access it:

```
var page = require('webpage').create();
page.open('http://localhost:8080/', function (status) {
});
```

*The Web Server module*

Use this module to listen and proxy transactions between the web page and remote resources. You can also use the Web Server module to output to a local port. Use the following to access it:

```
var webserver = require('webserver');
var server = webserver.create();
var service = server.listen('127.0.0.1', function(request,
response) {
  });
```

*The File System module*

The File System module gives you access to local file system functionality such as reading and writing files and directories. To access this module, type the following:

```
var fs = require('fs');
var file = fs.open('[local file] ', '[Open mode]')
```

You can find the full API documentation for PhantomJS at *http://bit. ly/13DeMD2*.

With this in mind, here are a couple of things you would want to test by using PhantomJS:

- Are the appropriate assets being loaded based on the client capabilities?
- Are the payloads for each experience within our determined SLA?

Let's take a look at how you can use PhantomJS to achieve this.

### Evaluate experiential resource loading

The first test case we'll look at is ensuring that our page is loading the correct assets. We've already talked at length about why we want to serve only the assets that are appropriate to a given client device (to reduce size payload, account for different bandwidth qualities and levels of availability, and accommodate different viewport sizes), and we've looked at ways to accomplish this both from the backend and the frontend, but now we will look at how to programmatically verify that this is happening.

We can do this by spoofing the viewport size and or User Agent of our headless browser and then evaluating specific assets that are loaded on the page. In the example that follows, we will use the Web Page module to create a simulated page, set the viewport property (which accepts a JavaScript Object Notation (JSON) object for width and height values), and assign the userAgent property to make the web page and web server that is serving up the web page think that an iPhone 5 is making the request:

```
var page = require('webpage').create();
    //simulating an iPhone 5
    page.viewportSize = {
        width: 640,
        height: 1136
    };
    page.settings.userAgent = 'Mozilla/5.0 (iPad; CPU OS 4_3_5
like Mac OS X; en-us) AppleWebKit/533.17.9 (KHTML, like Gecko)
Version/5.0.2 Mobile/8L1 Safari/6533.18.5';
    page.zoomFactor = 1;
    page.open('http://localhost:8080/', function (status) {

    });
```

We want to validate that the page is rendering as it should and with the appropriate content. We can do this several ways:

- Take a screenshot of the rendered page to visually confirm, usually in a manual fashion, that the expected layout is rendered. The code snippet that follows opens a web page, checks to ensure it was opened successfully, and saves a screenshot by using the page.render function:

```
page.open('http://localhost:8080/', function
(status) {
        if(status == 'success'){
page.render('./screenshots/iPhone5.png');
}
    });
```

- Programmatically examine the page elements to see if the assets that we expect to be rendered are actually rendered. In the code snippet that follows, on successful page loading, the page.evaluate function retrieves the URI in the src attribute of the element that has an id of description-image. Assuming we are still evaluating the iPhone 5 experience, we then check this URI to see if it is being loaded from the directory that we know holds the size-appropriate resources:

```
page.open('http://localhost:8080/', function (status) {
        if(status == 'success'){
var image_source = page.evaluate(function(s) {
    return document.querySelector(s).src;
  }, 'description-image');
  if (image_source){
…

}
}
    });
```

- Inspect the network requests that the web page makes to validate that the expected resources, and only the expected resources, are being downloaded. In the code snippet that follows, we create callback functions to capture HTTP requests that the page is making. Assuming we are still validating only the iPhone 5 scenario, each request fires off an anonymous function that will inspect the path to the resource to check to see if it is coming from a path that is known to hold images that are device inappropriate; for example, does the path contain the directory /nav/320/?

```
    page.onResourceRequested = function (request) {
        //check request to see if the requested resource is
coming from a known device
// inappropriate directory
    };

    page.open(address, function (status) { … });
```

### Validate web performance

So far, we've just looked at validating that what we are expecting to be downloaded and rendered in the page is actually there. Next, we will look at capturing the web performance of our web page in each experience. There are several ways we could do that:

- Within Phantom, measure how much time elapses between requesting a page and when the page completes rendering. The following code snippet takes a snapshot of the current time before calling the page. When the page is loaded, it takes another snapshot of the time and subtracts the start time from that to determine the page load time:

```
    var startTime = Date.now(),
        loadTime;

    page.open(address, function (status) {
    if (status == 'success') {
        loadTime = Date.now() - startTime;
        console.log("page load time: " + loadTime + "ms")
        }
    });
```

- Use YSlow for PhantomJS to generate a YSlow report. Yahoo! has created their own PhantomJS JavaScript file to make their YSlow services available from the command line. It is called *yslow.js* and is available at *http://yslow.org/phantomjs/*. Using *yslow.js* we can pass in specific User Agents to use, as well as viewport sizes. We can also pass in the format that we want the data to be output as well as the level of detail in the data. Figure 6-3 presents a screenshot of the succinct help section for *yslow.js*.

Figure 6-3 shows all of the arguments that the script accepts and even some example usage. This Help screen is also available at the command line by typing `phantomjs yslow.js –help`.

# Help

```
$ phantomjs yslow.js --help


Usage: phantomjs [phantomjs options] yslow.js [yslow options] [url ...]

PhantomJS Options:

  http://y.ahoo.it/phantomjs/options

YSlow Options:

  -h, --help                output usage information
  -V, --version             output the version number
  -i, --info <info>         specify the information to display/log (basic|grade|st
  -f, --format <format>     specify the output results format (json|xml|plain|tap|
  -r, --ruleset <ruleset>   specify the YSlow performance ruleset to be used (ydef
  -b, --beacon <url>        specify an URL to log the results
  -d, --dict                include dictionary of results fields
  -v, --verbose             output beacon response information
  -t, --threshold <score>   for test formats, the threshold to test scores ([0-100
                            e.g.: -t B or -t 75 or -t '{"overall": "B", "ycdn": "F
  -u, --ua "<user agent>"   specify the user agent string sent to server when the
  -vp, --viewport <WxH>     specify page viewport size WxY, where W = width and H
  -ch, --headers <JSON>     specify custom request headers, e.g.: -ch '{"Cookie":
  -c, --console <level>     output page console messages (0: none, 1: message, 2:
  --cdns "<list>"           specify comma separated list of additional CDNs

Examples:

  phantomjs yslow.js http://yslow.org
  phantomjs yslow.js -i grade -f xml www.yahoo.com www.cnn.com www.nytimes.com
  phantomjs yslow.js --info all --format plain --ua "MSIE 9.0" http://yslow.org
  phantomjs yslow.js -i basic --ruleset yslow1 -d http://yslow.org
  phantomjs yslow.js -i grade -b http://www.showslow.com/beacon/yslow/ -v yslow.o
  phantomjs --load-plugins=yes yslow.js -vp 800x600 http://www.yahoo.com
  phantomjs yslow.js -i grade -f tap -t 85 http://yslow.org
```

**FIGURE 6-3**

The Help section for YSlow.js

To continue with our example of testing our iPhone 5 experience, let's pass in our User Agent and viewport height and width, as shown in the following example:

```
> phantomjs yslow.js --info stats --format plain --vp 640x1136
--ua 'Mozilla/5.0 (iPad; CPU OS 4_3_5 like Mac OS X; en-us)
AppleWebKit/533.17.9 (KHTML, like Gecko) Version/5.0.2 Mo-
bile/8L1 Safari/6533.18.5' http://localhost:8080
version: 3.1.8
size: 846.4K (846452 bytes)
overall score: B (86)
```

```
url: http://localhost:8080/
# of requests: 46
ruleset: ydefault
page load time: 187
page size (primed cache): 10.2K (10290 bytes)
# of requests (primed cache): 1
statistics by component:
    doc:
        # of requests: 1
        size: 10.2K (10290 bytes)
    css:
        # of requests: 8
        size: 154.7K (154775 bytes)
    js:
        # of requests: 20
        size: 617.0K (617056 bytes)
    cssimage:
        # of requests: 6
        size: 32.6K (32694 bytes)
    image:
        # of requests: 10
        size: 14.0K (14095 bytes)
    favicon:
        # of requests: 1
        size: 17.5K (17542 bytes)
statistics by component (primed cache):
    doc:
        # of requests: 1
        size: 10.2K (10290 bytes)
```

Note the level of detail exposed: we get total payload of the page, the number of HTTP requests, and then a breakdown of number of HTTP requests and total payload by content type.

There are other alternatives to *YSlow.js* that work in much the same manner (e.g., James Pearce's *confess.js*, which you can get at *http://bit.ly/1ofAru5*).

In both use cases, remember that the intent would be to run through all of the different experiences for which we are accounting. Imagine for a moment that the tests that we just talked about were built in to your CI workflow, and your team was alerted every time a change was made that broke your service-level agreement. Let's make that a reality by next looking at how we can work these verification steps into a CI workflow.

## Continuous Integration

CI is the practice of real-time merging and testing of code check-ins. CI originally started life as a tenet of Kent Beck's *Extreme Programming* methodology, but it has spread to become the de facto practice of integrating changes within teams of developers. It follows the same principle as Beck's other best-known (and equally as ubiquitous) practice—test-driven development—in that moving the feedback loop closer to the resolver (in both cases the developer checking in code) saves both time and effort downstream in the process.

The core workflow of CI is to check in code and then follow these steps:

1. Confirm that the project builds (ensure that it compiles, or that the static content gets *minified* and gzipped, or that assets are renamed with a timestamp fingerprint for cache busting); if it does not, the build breaks

2. Run the integration and unit tests, and if they fail, break the build

Breaking the build should involve messaging out to the team and would require a code check-in to fix the cause of the build breakage. Figure 6-4 illustrates this workflow.

There are a number of software solutions that exist today to manage the workflow shown in Figure 6-4. One of the most popular among them is Jenkins. The beauty of Jenkins is that it is open source and easy to install and configure. A little later in this chapter, we will look at integrating our PhantomJS scripts into the CI workflow by using Jenkins.

First, however, we will take the concepts we just covered and make a script that we can run from Jenkins.

### AN EXAMPLE PHANTOMJS SCRIPT

To integrate your performance tests into Jenkins, we need to do several things. To begin, you must create a JavaScript file that will evaluate your performance SLAs. This file will output by using the JSUnit XML format, which Jenkins can easily read in. Jenkins will run this script and generate the XML file during each build, and it will read in the XML file as the test results after each build.

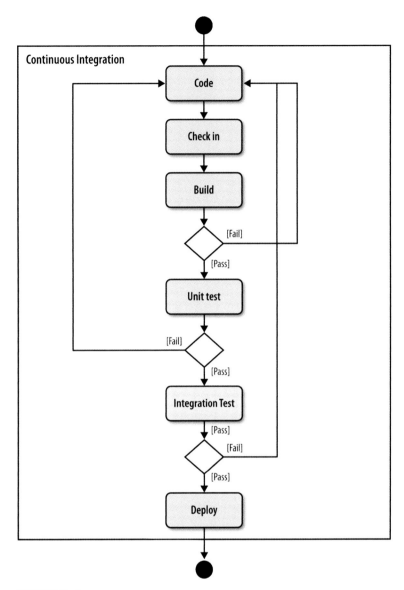

**FIGURE 6-4**
A CI work flow

**[ TIP ]**

Before we begin creating the script, we are going to add *async.js* to our project, which will make it possible for us to run our tests asynchronously. When we try to capture how long a page takes to load while we add up the byte size of each asset as they get downloaded, the act of interfacing with assets as they are downloading would add latency to the overall page load time and give us inaccurate results for that particular test.

To install *async.js*, go to the *project* directory and type `npm install async`.

This creates the directory structure shown in Figure 6-5 within our project and makes async available to our code.

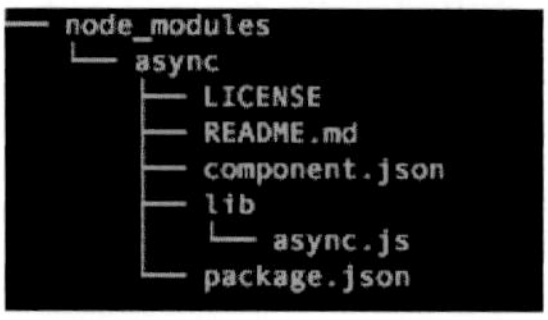

node_modules
async
LICENSE
README.md
component.json
lib
async.js
package.json


**FIGURE 6-5**
Tree view of the async module in the project directory

OK, let's begin. First, we'll create the variables that we will be using. We will load async into a variable that we will call `async`. Next, we'll create an array named `testsToRun` with the names of the tests that we will be running—for this example, `rendertime` and `payload`. Finally, we will create an object named `results` that will hold the values of each of the tests, including the human-readable display name for each test, the threshold for each test, and the actual results of the tests.

For readability purposes, this example hard codes several items. For an actual production script, you would seek to move all of the hardcoded values to be configurable and read in at runtime. Let's look at the code:

```
var async = require('async'),
    testsToRun = ["rendertime","payload"],
    results = {
        testnames:{
            rendertime:"Time to Render",
            payload: "Total Page Payload"
        },
```

```
            threshold: {
                rendertime: 500,
                payload: 1000
            },
            actual: {
                rendertime: 0,
                payload:0
            },
            test_results: {
                rendertime: "fail",
                payload: "fail"
            }
        }
    }
```

Next, create a function called test. This will encapsulate all of the tests that we will be running. We will pass in the test type and a callback function. We pass in the test type so that we can determine which tests to run at a given invocation. We pass in the callback function so that we can call it after our tests are complete; this way, async knows that the function invocation is complete.

Within the test function, first declare some variables and values. We will capture a snapshot of the current time, load the WebPage module into a variable named page, and we will hardcode the viewport as well as the User Agent. Again, the hardcoded values would normally be configurable at runtime, but for the sake of having an example that is easy to follow, they are hardcoded here:

```
function test(testType, callback){
    var startTime = Date.now(),
        loadTime;
    var page = require('webpage').create();
    page.viewportSize = {
            width: 640,
            height: 1136
        };

        page.settings.userAgent = 'Mozilla/5.0 (iPad; CPU OS
    4_3_5 like Mac OS X; en-us) AppleWebKit/533.17.9 (KHTML, like
    Gecko) Version/5.0.2 Mobile/8L1 Safari/6533.18.5';
        page.zoomFactor = 1;
    }
```

Next, within the test function, create the onResourceReceived event handler for the page object. This executes when remote resources that have been requested are received. Within this function, we will check to see whether any other tests to measure the page payload are under way (so that we don't add latency to those other tests), and if so, we then increment the payload property in the `results.actual` object:

```
page.onResourceReceived = function (resp) {
//increment the payload by the size of the resource received
    if(testType == "payload"){
        if(resp.bodySize != undefined){
                results.actual.payload += resp.bodySize
        }
    }
};
```

While still within the test function, call the `page.open` function to load the web page that is being performance tested. For our purposes, we will hardcode a local address, but in reality this should also be configurable at runtime. After the page is loaded, we capture the current time, and subtract the start time from that to establish the actual render time. We then call a function which we will define momentarily that uses the name `calculateResults`. Finally, we close the page and call the callback function to signal async that the function is complete:

```
page.open('http://localhost:8080/', function (status) {
if(status == 'success'){
    results.actual.rendertime = Date.now() - startTime;
}
calculateResults()
page.close();
callback.apply();
});
```

Before we leave the test function, let's define `calculateResults`. In this function, we'll us `testType` as the index and compare the actual test results with the threshold and then assign a passing or failing grade to the results property:

```
function calculateResults(){
if(results.actual[testType] <= results.threshold[testType]){
    results.test_results[testType] = "pass";
}
}
```

OK, returning to the root of our script, let's add the controller logic. Using `async.each`, we asynchronously call the test function with each value in the `testsToRun` array. When the function calls are complete, the anonymous function that we pass in as the third parameter to `asynch.each` executes. This function calls a function `formatOutput` that we will define shortly, and then exits PhantomJS:

```
async.each(testsToRun,test,
    function(err){
        formatOutput();
        phantom.exit();
    }
);
```

Finally, let's define a function called `formatOutput`. This function formats our output to adhere to the JUnit XML format that Jenkins accepts. We can find the XSD for this format at *http://bit.ly/Ze98o9*.

For the purposes of this exercise, we'll just create a suite for all of our tests and then a test case for each test that ran. We'll map a function to the array `testsToRun` to create test case nodes for each test. After we have the output assembled, we'll output it to the console:

```
function formatOutput(){
    var output = '<?xml version="1.0" encoding="utf-8"?>\n'+
    '<testsuite tests="'+ testsToRun.length +'">\n'
    testsToRun.map(function(t){
        output += '<testcase classname="'+ t +'" name="'+
results.testnames[t] +'">\n'
        if(results.test_results[t] == "fail"){
            output += '<failure type="fail"> threshold: '+
results.threshold[t] + ' result: '+ results.actual[t] +' </
failure>\n'
        }
        output += '</testcase>\n'
    })
    output += '</testsuite>'
    console.log(output)
}
```

Following is the complete code for this example (you can also find it on GitHub at *https://github.com/tomjbarker/HP_ResponsiveDesign*):

```
//simulating an iPhone 5
var async = require('async'),
    testsToRun = ["rendertime","payload"],
    results = {
        testnames:{
            rendertime:"Time to Render",
            payload: "Total Page Payload"
        },
        threshold: {
            rendertime: 500,
            payload: 1000
        },
```

```javascript
                actual: {
                    rendertime: 0,
                    payload:0
                },
                test_results: {
                    rendertime: "fail",
                    payload: "fail"
                }
        }

    function test(testType, callback){
        var startTime = Date.now(),
            loadTime;

        var page = require('webpage').create();
        page.viewportSize = {
                width: 640,
                height: 1136
            };

            page.settings.userAgent = 'Mozilla/5.0 (iPad; CPU OS
    4_3_5 like Mac OS X; en-us) AppleWebKit/533.17.9 (KHTML, like
    Gecko) Version/5.0.2 Mobile/8L1 Safari/6533.18.5';
            page.zoomFactor = 1;

            page.onResourceReceived = function (resp) {
                //increment the payload by the size of the re-
    source received
                if(testType == "payload"){
                    if(resp.bodySize != undefined){
                        results.actual.payload += resp.bodySize
                    }

                }
            };

            page.open('http://localhost:8080/', function (status)
    {

            if(status == 'success'){
                results.actual.rendertime = Date.now() - start-
    Time;
            }
            calculateResults()
            page.close();
            callback.apply();
            });

            function calculateResults(){
                var output = "";
                if(results.actual[testType] <= results.thresh-
    old[testType]){
```

```javascript
                        results.test_results[testType] = "pass";
                    }
                }
        }

        function formatOutput(){
            var output = '<?xml version="1.0" encoding="utf-8"?>\n'+
            '<testsuite tests="'+ testsToRun.length +'">\n'
            testsToRun.map(function(t){
                    output += '<testcase classname="'+ t +'" name="'+
        results.testnames[t] +'">\n'
                    if(results.test_results[t] == "fail"){
                            output += '<failure type="fail"> threshold: '+
        results.threshold[t] + ' result: '+ results.actual[t] +' </
        failure>\n'
                    }
                    output += '</testcase>\n'
            })
            output += '</testsuite>'
            console.log(output)
        }

        async.each(testsToRun,test,
          function(err){
                formatOutput();
                phantom.exit();
          }
        );
```

Save the script to a file named *iphone5test.js* and run it from the Terminal. You should see output similar to that shown in Figure 6-6.

**FIGURE 6-6**
Our script running in the Terminal (notice the output in JUnit XML format)

Next, we will install Jenkins and get our script running in the build process for a project.

## JENKINS

Jenkins started life as Hudson, an open source CI tool created by Kohsuke Kawaguchi while at Sun Microsystems. After Oracle purchased Sun, the Jenkins CI project split off from Hudson. Hudson would continue under Oracle's stewardship (Oracle eventually transferred the project to the Eclipse Foundation), whereas Jenkins CI would continue on through the contributions of the community.

Jenkins is available from *http://jenkins-ci.org/*, where you can, among other things, download the latest build, create your own copy, register a bug, or read documentation around Jenkins. Figure 6-7 presents the Jenkins CI home page.

**FIGURE 6-7**

The Jenkins CI home page

From the Jenkins home page, you can download a native package to install. In Figure 6-8, you can see the installer for Mac OS.

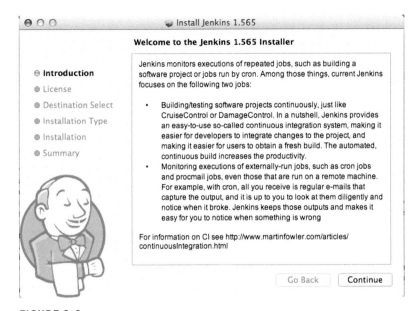

**FIGURE 6-8**
The Jenkins Mac OS installer

After you've completed installation, Jenkins is available locally at *http://localhost:8080/*, as demonstrated in Figure 6-9.

**FIGURE 6-9**
The Jenkins home page following a fresh installation

For this example, we will assume that the GitHub plug-in is installed (if it isn't, go to Manage Jenkins, click Manage Plugins, and then install it) and that we are using GitHub as our source control.

To begin, we need to have a project in Jenkins. To create a new project, on the Jenkins home page, click New Item. A window similar to that depicted in Figure 6-10 opens. For our example, we will create a free-style project and give it a name.

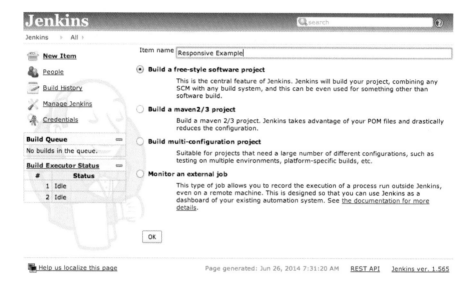

**FIGURE 6-10**
Creating a new project in Jenkins

Now, it's time to configure the new project. On the Source Code Management page, choose Git as the source code management technology and type the location of our project in GitHub, as depicted in Figure 6-11.

Next, we add a build step to execute our PhantomJS script, with the output piped to an XML file called *results.xml* (see Figure 6-12). This runs our script and generates a new XML file every time the project is built.

Finally, while still on the Source Code Management page, add a post-build action to publish the JUnit test result report, or specifically the *results.xml* file that we created with our script (see Figure 6-13).

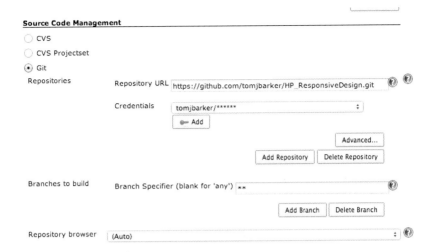

FIGURE 6-11

Pointing our Jenkins project to our GitHub project

FIGURE 6-12

Running our PhantomJS script from the shell during the build process and
piping the output to an XML file

FIGURE 6-13

Reading in the XML that was generated during the build as a post-build test

From here, we can manually kick off builds from Jenkins, and our script is run and the report is generated. If we want our project to build every time we push a change to GitHub, we would need to configure a web hook in GitHub to POST to our Jenkins installation.

After the build runs, we can see the for the web performance test in Jenkins. Figure 6-14 shows the results.

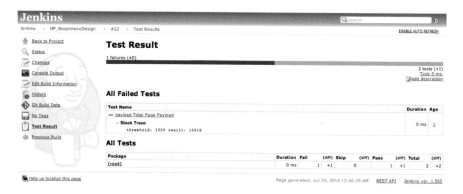

**FIGURE 6-14**
Results of our tests output in Jenkins!

With this flow in place, we can now get real-time feedback as changes we make in the code base impact our web performance.

## Summary

This chapter explored continuous web performance testing. We looked at using PhantomJS to create headless browser tests. We talked at length about how to verify that the patterns of best practice that we established in previous chapters were being maintained, from loading only device-specific assets, to maintaining a page payload and render-time SLA.

Finally, we looked at incorporating that logic into a CI workflow using Jenkins.

Chapter 7 takes a survey of the current state of frameworks addressing the issues of performant responsive websites.

# [ 7 ]

# Frameworks

## Looking at the State of Responsive Frameworks

So far, we have looked at web performance patterns and anti-patterns in the world of responsive design. We've looked at crafting our own solutions to implement these patterns of best practices, both from the client side and the server side. Chapter 6 shows how to create automated tests via PhantomJS to verify the adherence to our performance-responsive design patterns and include them in a continuous integration (CI) workflow using Jenkins. In this chapter, we will explore some of the frameworks that are available, and analyze how they handle web performance. Different types of responsive frameworks exist: there are boilerplates that give predetermined page layouts; there are grid systems that just define responsive grid layouts; and then there are complete solutions that include different page layouts with reusable modules, web fonts, and JavaScript functionality.

If you look at the overall landscape of frameworks, the first thing you'll note is that they are all implemented for the frontend. In these frameworks, there will generally be predefined CSS that describes the styling of a module such as a button or a grid, or even complex UI elements such as accordions and sliders and guided navigation. You can use these modules by assigning their classes to elements on your page. Some frameworks have a JavaScript API with which you can programmatically create styled elements on your page.

As of this writing, the biggest names in frameworks are Twitter's Bootstrap and Foundation from ZURB. In fact, when we look at Google Trend to compare relative search interest in Bootstrap and Foundation to other frameworks, we need to create two different charts because the interest in Bootstrap is a full order of magnitude greater than interest in the other frameworks, which is amply illustrated in Figures 7-1 and 7-2.

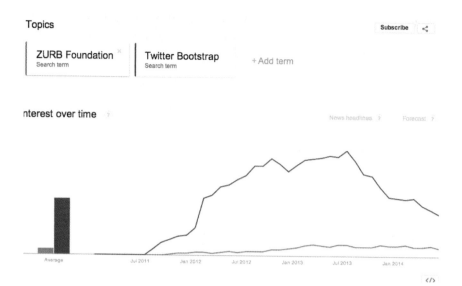

**FIGURE 7-1**

Comparing relative search interest between Twitter Bootstrap and ZURB's Foundation framework

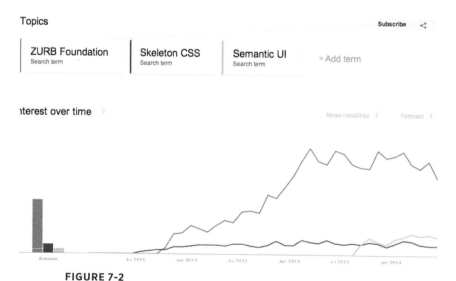

**FIGURE 7-2**

Comparing relative search interest in ZURB's Foundation, Skeleton, and Semantic UI

In Figures 7-1 and 7-2, note the difference in scale between the two Google Trend images, with Foundation being the common link between the two charts (the blue line in both charts).

We will begin by establishing criteria that we will be using to evaluate these frameworks.

Our criteria will be the following:

What patterns and/or anti-patterns does the framework use?

How easy is it to use?

What is the size of the framework, including dependencies?

What, if any, dependencies does the framework have, including dependencies on other frameworks or libraries?

Let's commence the evaluation by first looking at Twitter's Bootstrap.

## Twitter Bootstrap

Bootstrap is a frontend, open source framework created in 2011 by Mark Otto and Jacob Thornton at Twitter and is available at *http://getbootstrap.com/*. Figure 7-3 shows the Bootstrap home page.

Bootstrap's base installation comes with predefined CSS and JavaScript to implement a set of frontend components that have responsiveness built in to them. These components include buttons, tabs, progress bars, grid systems, patterns for alerts, and even specific page layouts.

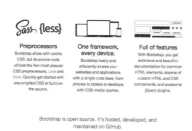

**FIGURE 7-3**

The Bootstrap homepage

The install consists of the directory structure, which you can see in Figure 7-4.

```
├── css
│   ├── bootstrap-theme.css
│   ├── bootstrap-theme.css.map
│   ├── bootstrap-theme.min.css
│   ├── bootstrap.css
│   ├── bootstrap.css.map
│   └── bootstrap.min.css
├── fonts
│   ├── glyphicons-halflings-regular.eot
│   ├── glyphicons-halflings-regular.svg
│   ├── glyphicons-halflings-regular.ttf
│   └── glyphicons-halflings-regular.woff
└── js
    ├── bootstrap.js
    └── bootstrap.min.js
```

**FIGURE 7-4**
The core Bootstrap installation

Using Bootstrap is as simple as including the core CSS and JavaScript files on your page, and then you begin using predefined components. Also note that Bootstrap requires JQuery:

```
<link href="css/bootstrap.min.css" rel="stylesheet">
<script src="js/bootstrap.min.js"></script>
<script src="https://ajax.googleapis.com/ajax/libs/jquery/
1.11.1/jquery.min.js"></script>
```

It's easy to see why Bootstrap is so popular: in around 20 minutes, using the built-in components and styles from Bootstrap, I was able to construct the website shown in Figure 7-5 (it's available at *http://tom-jbarker.github.io/*).

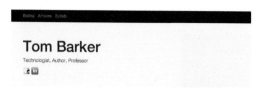

**FIGURE 7-5**

An example website created in Bootstrap

## EVALUATION

Take a look at Table 7-1 to see how Bootstrap fared in our evaluation.

**TABLE 7-1.** Evaluating Bootstrap

| | |
|---|---|
| PATTERNS/ANTI-PATTERNS | Out of the box, Bootstrap will load the same assets for each experience. Images will be resized on the client side to fit the viewport. There are JQuery plug-ins that you can use to somewhat address this. A popular one is HiSRC (available at *https://github.com/teleject/hisrc*), that loads a smaller, mobile-friendly image first and then, depending on the connection speed and the client device pixel ratio, loads additional larger images. Though this fixes the small-screen scenario, in that it loads a device-specific asset, it then must load additional assets for larger screen experiences. |
| EASE OF USE | Using existing Bootstrap modules and styling, I was able to construct a responsive website in less than 20 minutes. |
| DEPENDENCIES | JQuery |
| SIZE OF THE FRAMEWORK (AND DEPENDENCIES) | The minimum installation requires Bootstrap's CSS and JavaScript as well as JQuery. As of this writing, the totals for these are:<br><br>*bootstrap.min.css*: 107 KB<br><br>*jquery.min.js*: 82.6 KB<br><br>*bootstrap.min.js*: 31KB<br><br>------------------------------------<br><br>Grand total: 220.6 KB<br><br>Keep in mind that this is just the minimum installation. There are themes and web fonts that you might also want to use which would add to that total. |

# ZURB Foundation

The next framework we will evaluate is Foundation by ZURB, a design firm from California. Foundation was created and made available as open source in 2011. You can download it from *http://foundation.zurb.com/*. Figure 7-6 depicts the Foundation home page.

**FIGURE 7-6**

The home page for ZURB Foundation

Downloading and unzipping the framework creates the directory structure shown in Figure 7-7.

```
├── css
│   ├── foundation.css
│   ├── foundation.min.css
│   └── normalize.css
├── humans.txt
├── img
├── index.html    ─
├── js
│   ├── foundation
│   │   ├── foundation.abide.js
│   │   ├── foundation.accordion.js
│   │   ├── foundation.alert.js
│   │   ├── foundation.clearing.js
│   │   ├── foundation.dropdown.js
│   │   ├── foundation.equalizer.js
│   │   ├── foundation.interchange.js
│   │   ├── foundation.joyride.js
│   │   ├── foundation.js
│   │   ├── foundation.magellan.js
│   │   ├── foundation.offcanvas.js
│   │   ├── foundation.orbit.js
│   │   ├── foundation.reveal.js
│   │   ├── foundation.slider.js
│   │   ├── foundation.tab.js
│   │   ├── foundation.tooltip.js
│   │   └── foundation.topbar.js
│   ├── foundation.min.js
│   └── vendor
│       ├── fastclick.js
│       ├── jquery.cookie.js
│       ├── jquery.js
│       ├── modernizr.js
│       └── placeholder.js
└── robots.txt
```

**FIGURE 7-7**
Tree view of the Foundation installation

Just like Bootstrap, Foundation comes with prestyled components, including media queries to handle different viewport sizes. Also, like Bootstrap, pages are arranged in rows and columns with CSS classes assigned to <div>s to specify explicit grid structure and which component to load.

Using the built-in components from Foundation, I constructed the website presented in Figure 7-8. You can look at the site at *http://bit.ly/1ORjT1n*. Table 7-2 provides the evaluation data.

**Tom Barker**

Technologist, Author, Professor

Books    Articles    Syllabi

**Books**

**Articles**

| Safari Online | dotNet Magazine | IBM |
|---|---|---|
| A DATA VISUALIZATION PRIMER | WHY DATA IS YOUR GREATEST ASSET (AFTER PEOPLE) | VISUALIZE IN-BROWSER PERFORMANCE DATA WITH R AND JAVASCRIPT USING THE W3C PERFORMANCE OBJECT |
| INTRO TO R WITH DATA VISUALIZATION | | DATA VISUALIZATION WITH R: HOW TO GET AND SHOW MEANINGFUL METRICS FOR A SCRUM TEAM |
| INTRO TO D3: A DATA VISUALIZATION PRIMER | | |
| INTRO TO D3JS JS: A DATA VISUALIZATION PRIMER | | |
| INTRO TO PROCESSING JS: A DATA VISUALIZATION PRIMER | | |
| INTRO TO PLOT: A DATA VISUALIZATION PRIMER | | |
| READING AND PARSING EXTERNAL DATA IN R | | |
| OBJECT ORIENTED PROGRAMMING IN R: PART 1, S3 OBJECTS | | |
| OBJECT ORIENTED PROGRAMMING IN R: PART 2, S4 OBJECTS | | |
| R STUDIO, R MARKDOWN, AND DISTRIBUTING YOUR R SCRIPTS ON THE WEB USING RPUBS | | |
| CRAFTING DATA MAPS IN R | | |
| IMPLEMENTING PIE CHARTS IN R | | |

**Syllabi**

**Philadelphia University**

DATA VISUALIZATION WITH JAVASCRIPT AND R

DATABASE MANAGEMENT AND SCRIPTING

WEB DEVELOPMENT

INTRO TO ACTIONSCRIPT 3

**FIGURE 7-8**

A website created by using Foundation

Let's look at how Foundation fared, see Table 7-2.

**TABLE 7-2.** Evaluating Foundation

| PATTERNS/ANTI-PATTERNS | Same assets loaded for every experience, images resized client-side |
|---|---|
| EASE OF USE | Same as Bootstrap, using the prepackaged modules |
| DEPENDENCIES | Modernizr, JQuery |
| SIZE OF THE FRAMEWORK (AND DEPENDENCIES) | *foundation.css*: 153.6 KB |
| | *modernizr.js*: 11 KB |
| | *jquery.js*: 82.6 KB |
| | *foundation.js*: (minified) 89.9 KB |
| | ------------------------------------- |
| | Grand total: 337.1 KB |

## Skeleton

Skeleton was created and released in 2011 by Dave Gamache, formerly of Twitter. You can download it from *http://www.getskeleton.com/*. Figure 7-9 shows the Skeleton home page.

**Skeleton**

# A Beautiful Boilerplate for Responsive, Mobile-Friendly Development

## What Is It?

Skeleton is a small collection of CSS files that can help you rapidly develop sites that look beautiful at any size, be it a 17˝ laptop screen or an iPhone. Skeleton is built on three core principles:

**Responsive Grid Down To Mobile**
Skeleton has a familiar, lightweight 960 grid as its base, but elegantly scales down to downsized browser windows, tablets, mobile phones (in landscape and portrait). **Go ahead, resize this page!**

**Fast to Start**
Skeleton is a tool for rapid development. Get started fast with CSS best practices, a well-structured grid that makes mobile consideration easy, an organized file structure and super basic UI elements like lightly styled forms, buttons, tabs and more.

**Style Agnostic**
Skeleton is not a UI framework. It's a development kit that provides the most basic styles as a foundation, but is ready to adopt whatever your design or style is.

**FIGURE 7-9**

The Skeleton home page with instructions and inline code examples

If you download and unzip the Skeleton framework, you can see that it is more of a boilerplate, with an *index.html* page for us to edit and an existing directory hierarchy with the necessary CSS and images that the code references. Figure 7-10 illustrates the unzipped Skeleton directory tree structure.

**FIGURE 7-10**
Skeleton website boilerplate, unzipped

Whereas Bootstrap comes with prestyled components such as the Jumbotron, Skeleton takes a much more minimalist approach. There is barely any styling to speak of; mainly it offers just buttons, forms, and typography, along with layout definitions. The idea is to use Skeleton for minimal layout and layer your own styles on top of it.

Using the included boilerplate, you can construct a website similar in structure to the previous examples, styled in in the minimalist vein of Skeleton, as shown in Figure 7-11. You can obtain Skeleton at *http://tomjbarker.github.io/skeleton/*.

# Tom Barker
Technologist, Author, Professor

## Books

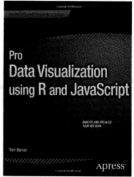

## Articles

### Safari Online

A Data Visualization Primer
Intro to R with Data Visualization
Intro to D3: A Data Visualization Primer
Intro to InfoVis: A Data Visualization Primer
Intro to Processing js: A Data Visualization Primer
Intro to Flot: A Data Visualization Primer
Reading and Parsing External Data in R
Object-Oriented Programming in R: Part 1, S3 Objects
Object Oriented Programming in R: Part 2, S4 Objects
RStudio, R Markdown, and Distributing Your R Scripts on the Web using RPubs
Crafting Data Maps in R
Implementing Pie Charts in R

### dotNet Magazine

Why data is your greatest asset (after people)

### IBM

Visualize in-browser performance data with R and JavaScript using the W3C performance object
Data visualization with R: How to get and show meaningful metrics for a scrum team

## Syllabi

### Philadelphia University

Data Visualization with JavaScript and R
Database Management and Scripting
Web Development
Intro to ActionScript 3

**FIGURE 7-11**

A website created by using Skeleton

**EVALUATION**

Let's see how Skeleton fared in our evaluation criteria, see Table 7-3.

**TABLE 7-3.** Evaluating Skeleton

| | |
|---|---|
| PATTERNS/ANTI-PATTERNS | Skeleton loads the same assets for all device experiences. The upside is that there is so little to the framework that it is the smallest possible footprint anyway. |
| EASE OF USE | Easy-to-use, baked-in styles, but if you want to have any sort of styling you must add your own. |
| DEPENDENCIES | None |
| SIZE OF THE FRAMEWORK (AND DEPENDENCIES) | Skeleton really is a minimal install. We only need two of the CSS files that come with the install, *base.css* and *skeleton.css*. These files don't come minified, but for my example I minified them. The totals for these, at the time of this writing, are: *base.css*: (minified) 6.1KB *skeleton.css*: (minified) 5.4 KB *layout.css*: 1.7 KB ------------------------------------- Grand total: 13.2 KB Keep in mind that this doesn't count any styling we might want to layer on top of Skeleton. And, unless you want the bare minimum of design (any you might actually want that), you will need to add additional styling. |

## Semantic UI

Semantic UI is another web framework, again implemented on the frontend, that provides prestyled UI components with client-side responsiveness built in. It is available at *http://semantic-ui.com/*. Figure 7-12 presents a screenshot of the Semantic UI home page.

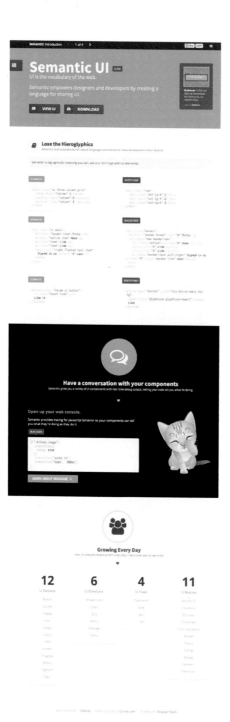

**FIGURE 7-12**

The Semantic UI home page

From the home page, you can download a ZIP file that contains the directory structures that shown in Figure 7-13. There is an examples directory that contains a couple of sample pages that demonstrate how to use the framework, a less directory that contains individual LESS files for each component, a minified directory that holds individual mini-fied CSS files for each component. There is also a packaged directory that contains all of the UI components and the JavaScript API aggre-gated into a single CSS and JavaScript file (plus the minified version of these packaged files). Figure 7-14 shows the contents of the packaged directory. Finally, there is an uncompressed directory that contains all of the individual components as (uncompressed) CSS files.

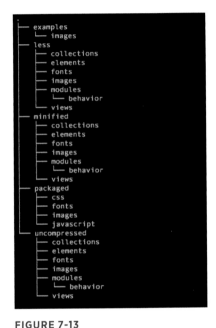

**FIGURE 7-13**

Tree view of the directories in the Semantic UI download

```
├── css
│   ├── semantic.css
│   └── semantic.min.css
├── fonts
│   ├── basic.icons.eot
│   ├── basic.icons.svg
│   ├── basic.icons.ttf
│   ├── basic.icons.woff
│   ├── icons.eot
│   ├── icons.otf
│   ├── icons.svg
│   ├── icons.ttf
│   └── icons.woff
├── images
│   ├── loader-large-inverted.gif
│   ├── loader-large.gif
│   ├── loader-medium-inverted.gif
│   ├── loader-medium.gif
│   ├── loader-mini-inverted.gif
│   ├── loader-mini.gif
│   ├── loader-small-inverted.gif
│   └── loader-small.gif
└── javascript
    ├── semantic.js
    └── semantic.min.js
```

**FIGURE 7-14**

Tree view of the packaged files from the Semantic UI download

In Figure 7-14, observe that the download also included CSS files for individual components so that we can choose to only utilize the files for the modules that we are using

Using the packaged CSS and based on the *homepage.html* example from the download, I was able to construct the example website displayed in Figure 7-15. The example is available at *http://tomjbarker.github.io/semantic/.*

**Tom Barker**
Technologist, Author, Professor

Books Articles Syllabi

## Books

## Articles

| Safari Online | dotNet Magazine | IBM |
|---|---|---|
| A DATA VISUALIZATION PRIMER | WHY DATA IS YOUR GREATEST ASSET (AFTER PEOPLE) | VISUALIZE IN BROWSER PERFORMANCE DATA WITH R AND JAVASCRIPT USING THE W3C PERFORMANCE OBJECT |
| INTRO TO R WITH DATA VISUALIZATION | | |
| INTRO TO D3: A DATA VISUALIZATION PRIMER | | DATA VISUALIZATION WITH R: HOW TO GET AND SHOW MEANINGFUL METRICS FOR A SCRUM TEAM |
| INTRO TO INFOVIS: A DATA VISUALIZATION PRIMER | | |
| INTRO TO PROCESSING JS: A DATA VISUALIZATION PRIMER | | |
| INTRO TO FLOT: A DATA VISUALIZATION PRIMER | | |
| READING AND PARSING EXTERNAL DATA IN R | | |
| OBJECT ORIENTED PROGRAMMING IN R: PART 1, S3 OBJECTS | | |
| OBJECT ORIENTED PROGRAMMING IN R: PART 2, S4 OBJECTS | | |
| RSTUDIO, R MARKDOWN, AND DISTRIBUTING YOUR R SCRIPTS ON THE WEB USING RPUBS | | |
| CRAFTING DATA MAPS IN R | | |
| IMPLEMENTING PIE CHARTS IN R | | |

## Syllabi

### Philadelphia University

DATA VISUALIZATION WITH JAVASCRIPT AND R

DATABASE MANAGEMENT AND SCRIPTING

WEB DEVELOPMENT

INTRO TO ACTIONSCRIPT 3

**FIGURE 7-15**

A website created using Semantic UI

## EVALUATION

Let's see how Semantic UI fared in our evaluation criteria (Table 7-4).

**TABLE 7-4.** Evaluating Semantic UI

| PATTERNS/ANTI-PATTERNS | Again, Semantic is a frontend framework that has all of the same anti-patterns with which we are all too familiar. |
|---|---|
| EASE OF USE | Same as Bootstrap and Foundation |
| DEPENDENCIES | JQuery |
| SIZE OF THE FRAMEWORK (AND DEPENDENCIES) | *semantic.css*: (minified) 231KB <br><br> *jquery.js*: 82.6 KB <br><br> *semantic.js*: (minified) 134.4 KB <br><br> ------------------------------------ <br><br> Grand total: 448 KB |

# A Comparison of Frontend Frameworks

When you compare the raw numbers, you can see that from the pool of frameworks that we've looked at, Semantic is the heaviest of the group—if you are using the packaged files and not cherry-picking components to include. Figure 7-16 provides a side-by-side comparison of the sheer size of the frameworks.

Figure 7-16 illustrates clearly that the sizes vary drastically, from 13 KB for Skeleton, up to 448 KB for Semantic UI. Taking this a step further, if you then look at the example websites using these frameworks—all with the same exact content—and look at the total payload for each site, breaking out the total payload for each asset type, you can see that the page size gets inflated from 460 KB, in the case of our Skeleton example, up to 907 KB for our Semantic UI example. Figure 7-17 depicts this break out.

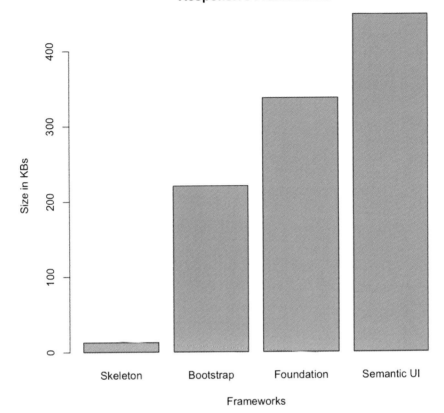

## Comparison of File Sizes of Responsive Frameworks

Size in KBs

**FIGURE 7-16**

Framework payload comparison

What is evident in Figure 7-17 is how the size of the frameworks impact the size of the overall page payload, where the red segments represents the size of the frameworks, whereas the blue segments represents the size of the HTML needed to create the pages, and the yellow segments represent the size of the images used in the pages. Notice that all the pages use the same images, and require roughly the same amount of HTML (within a 2 KB difference) to implement.

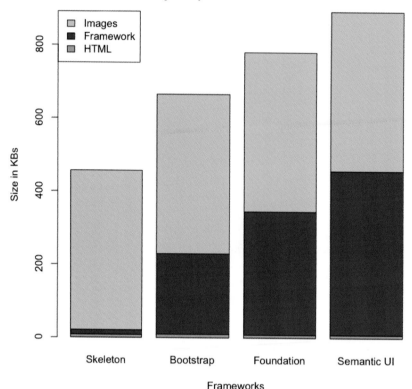

**FIGURE 7-17**

The impact of framework sizes on page payload

## Ripple

When I surveyed the landscape of responsive frameworks, it became clear to me that they are all frontend frameworks, and with the exception of Skeleton, they are not designed with performance in mind. Armed with this knowledge, I decided to create a bare-bones boiler-plate using NodeJS to set up a full-stack responsive website using the principles that we have been discussing in this book. I named the boil-erplate Ripple, and made it available for you at *https://github.com/tom jbarker/Ripple*. Following is the source code for Ripple:

```
var http = require("http");
var url = require("url");

var handle = {}
handle["/"] = checkUA;
handle["/favicon.ico"] = favicon;

var uaViewPortCategories = {
    "320": new RegExp(/Nexus S|iPhone|BB10|Nexus 4|Nexus 5|
HTC|LG|GT/),
    "640": new RegExp(/Nexus 7/),
    "1024": new RegExp(/Silk|iPad|Android/)
};

var assetPath = {
    "css": "assets/css/1024/",
    "img": "assets/img/1024/",
    "js": "assets/js/1024/"
};

var serv = http.createServer(function (req, res) {
    var pathname = url.parse(req.url).pathname;
    route(pathname, res, req);
});

function route(path, res, req){
    console.log("routing " + path);
    handle[path](res, req);
}

function checkUA(res, req) {
    var ua = req.headers["user-agent"]
    var re = new RegExp(/iPhone|iPod|iPad|Mobile|Android/);
    if(re.exec(ua)){
        getMobileCapabilities(ua, res);
    }
    renderExperience(res);
}


function getMobileCapabilities(ua, res){
    res.writeHead(200, { "Content-Type": "text/html" });
    var viewPortWidth = 1024;
    if(uaViewPortCategories["320"].exec(ua)){
        viewPortWidth = 320
    }else if(uaViewPortCategories["640"].exec(ua)){
        viewPortWidth = 640
    }else if(uaViewPortCategories["1024"].exec(ua)){
        viewPortWidth = 1024
    }
```

```
        assetPath.css = "assets/css/"+viewPortWidth+"/";
        assetPath.img = "assets/img/"+viewPortWidth+"/"
        assetPath.js = "assets/js/"+viewPortWidth+"/"
    }

    function renderExperience(res){
        res.writeHead(200, { "Content-Type": "text/html" });
        res.write(assetPath.css + "<br/>");
        res.write(assetPath.img + "<br/>");
        res.end(assetPath.js);
    }


    function favicon(res, req){
        res.writeHead(200, {
    'Content-Type': 'image/x-icon'
    } );
        res.end();
    }

    serv.listen(80);
```

To run the boilerplate, simply download the project from GitHub, change directory into the project directory, and then run the *engine.js* file from node, as follows:

```
node engine.js
```

The engine file checks the User Agent from the HTTP request, runs a series of regular expressions against the User Agent to determine the client, and based on the determination creates paths to static assets that are appropriate to the viewport size of the client device.

## Summary

As of this writing, all of the frameworks available are frontend frameworks. With the exception of Skeleton, most are heavy—some would say bloated—and all follow the same anti-patterns of loading the same assets for every device experience.

Again, as of this writing, there are no mainstream server-side frameworks or boilerplates available; if you are interested in what you've read so far and want to explore the concepts further, I hope you will check out Ripple and begin exploring the performance benefits that can be gained from focusing on responsiveness from the server side.

# [ *Index* ]

## [ *About the Author* ]

Tom Barker has been a software engineer since the '90s, focusing on the full stack of web development. Currently, he is Director of Software Development and Engineering at Comcast, an adjunct professor at Philadelphia University, a husband, a father, an amateur power lifter and armchair philosopher. He is obsessed with elegant software solutions, continual improvement, refining process, data analysis, and visualization.

# Have it your way.

# Get even more for your money.

## Join the O'Reilly Community, and register the O'Reilly books you own. It's free, and you'll get:

- $4.99 ebook upgrade offer
- 40% upgrade offer on O'Reilly print books
- Membership discounts on books and events
- Free lifetime updates to ebooks and videos
- Multiple ebook formats, DRM FREE
- Participation in the O'Reilly community
- Newsletters
- Account management
- 100% Satisfaction Guarantee

### Signing up is easy:

1. Go to: oreilly.com/go/register
2. Create an O'Reilly login.
3. Provide your address.
4. Register your books.

Note: English-language books only

**To order books online:**
oreilly.com/store

**For questions about products or an order:**
orders@oreilly.com

**To sign up to get topic-specific email announcements and/or news about upcoming books, conferences, special offers, and new technologies:**
elists@oreilly.com

**For technical questions about book content:**
booktech@oreilly.com

**To submit new book proposals to our editors:**
proposals@oreilly.com

**O'Reilly books are available in multiple DRM-free ebook formats. For more information:**
oreilly.com/ebooks